PERFECT LANDING
WRONG AIRPORT

*A Journey of a Black Woman in
Corporate South Africa*

DR ELLA FORD MTHETHWA

PERFECT LANDING WRONG AIRPORT

A Journey of a Black Woman in
Corporate South Africa

DR ELLA FORD MTHETHWA

Ellagence Enterprise (Pty) Ltd

Published in 2023 by Ellagence Enterprise (Pty) Ltd
Breyer Avenue.
Waverley
Pretoria
South Africa

ellagence@ellagence.com

Proofreading by Khethiwe Zulu
Cover Design by SeventhD Global Services
Foreword by Mrs Thulisile Galelekile
Inspirational Awakening by Sthandiwe Kgoroge
Life Coaching by Andrea Whitcher-Johnstone

Printed by Harry's Printers

CONTENTS

This book is dedicated to my friends and family who have
shown me unconditional love through the peaks and
troughs. They have been with me through my tumultuous
yet rewarding journey in my life as I worked for the corporate
world, encouraging me, and showing unwavering support
that motivated me to face the challenges as I continued to
stand for what is right.

I will forever be grateful to the people of all races
that I have met along the way who also have supported me.
They have enabled me to thrive and continuously strive
for excellence.

To my beloved parents Frank Charles and Ruth
Thozama Ford who taught me to believe in God and the
power of the cross, who instilled the values, integrity and
confidence which has enabled me to reach this milestone, I
love you, I thank you. Mbali and Mfundo Mthethwa, thank you
for the love and for keeping me sane and focused on every
dream I have endeavoured. Sis Gugu, Sis Mandi and Thando, your
prayers have carried me...

Finally, I dedicate this book to my Heavenly Father, my God, who
has guided me through my journey and this process. He has never
left me, and neither will He forsake me!

ELLA

AUTHOR'S NOTE

The author hereby states that the stories and information herein is shared to the best of her knowledge and memory of a journey. All the names, characters and businesses in this book are either the product of the author's imagination or used in a fictitious manner so as not to be identifiable. Any direct resemblance will be purely coincidental.

All terms referring to race are used to identify the characters in the various destinations based on the context of the relevant scenarios being set and are not to be offensive. This may include the inter-changeable use of such terms.

FOREWORD

This book is long overdue and what an honour to be part of a journey unfolding.

This is a true-life story many have been afraid to tell, yet that needs to be heard far and wide; the story of triumph over grave difficulties, for grave they are, designed to marginalize and to silence. This is a story of courage over setbacks; that of mastering the art of success against all odds.

This is a story of a journey to triumph, built over years of fighting to be recognized, to be seen and to take our rightful place at a table we should have never been 'chased' from. A story of succeeding over a system so riddled with fear that it opts to silence instead of embracing, for it does not want its boat rocked and disturbed for fear that we might shake the very foundation it has worked so hard to build and secure.

The time is now that this system must hear the crying voices of black women and take notice of the power and contribution we bring to the table, to take notice of the power in diversity and to appreciate that in this diversity comes success that transcends past hurdles and the test of time. I am therefore truly honoured to have been given an opportunity to contribute to this long-awaited project.

"Perfect Landing. Wrong Airport" comes at an opportune time in the world. We are at a crossroads of our awakening. We have just come through the most difficult time of the COVID pandemic that has turned our world upside down, forcing us to reflect and to question many things around us. A time of re-awakening of senses and most importantly our conscience, forcing us to look deep into our very soul and question who we are and why we are here. I am therefore not surprised that Dr Ella, a very good friend, has chosen this time to write this book and to compel corporate South Africa to reflect on their impact in our world. Our only hope is that this book will touch a few corporates, encouraging them to take stock of the way their systems are designed, and drive a change that is so needed by all of us.

The truth is, as black women in corporate we have always known who we are, our strength and our brilliance. We carry our brilliance with pride, and we continue to rise despite the difficulties faced. We have mastered the art of hiding the scars of years of pain and proving ourselves, commanding the room every time we walk in. This book is our compass, our light and an awakening that corporate needs to do if they still want to stand tall and be counted years after we are gone. This is a book of truth that needs to come out, told through the lens of one of our own successful sisters, our beacon of light.

I congratulate Dr Ella for raising this known fact, for carrying our torch as black women and showing the world what we are capable of, for being courageous to table a necessary topic if we are to prosper going forward. I commend her for being the conscience the world so needs, and for tackling the issue that will shine the spotlight on the plight of those that have been marginalized for too long. It is in the discomfort that we transverse into greatness.

Amandla Dr Ella! May this be the change we so need in South Africa.

THULISILE GALELEKILE.

INTRODUCTION

With every journey that we embark on as human beings there is an element of mystery and intrigue as to what it is that lies beyond the oceans, the rivers and valleys that separate our various "destinations". As we manoeuvre and make strategic moves in our careers, there is always a certain level of expectation that the next move will bring about more positive and much better experiences than before. While at first glance, this book might create an impression of being about the challenges of a traveller, it really is about the corporate journey of a black woman, where she landed, her negative experiences and how she managed to turn the learnings into victory.

The universal truth is that most human beings want to make a meaningful impact in this world, to leave a legacy. We are passers-by who want to leave this world better than we found it. As a humanitarian there is no part of my life where I have not been intentional in ensuring that I have touched the lives of those around me; including the corporate spaces where I have seen a need to intervene in challenging the injustices that prevail. This has been and continues to be my contribution, where it has been necessary. This book aims to reach further to all the corners of this world, resonating with every soul that has been through similar struggles and understands the challenges that present themselves in this journey, a journey that is life-changing for those regarded less than worthy. Suffice to say that the status remains the same in today's world for many. My hope is that they too will draw learnings and inspiration to make bold moves for change.

The title of the book comes from a heartfelt letter that I wrote to one of my employers where I experienced yet another wave of racist behaviour that was unexpected in terms of its intensity, given that at the time there was still the euphoria of the birth of the "Rainbow Nation", our "new" South Africa. This letter is presented in the last chapter of the book and will give context to the inception of this concept.

While this journey may evoke deep negative feelings as we travel together, and as I relive the emotional brutality that I can remember, it is by no means aimed at inciting violence or hatred. It is an honest account of what we see when we look at the rear-view mirrors of our careers, the truths lived and witnessed in our country, South Africa. These truths are revealed in pockets of some less told narratives of our people of this generation.

"Perfect Landing. Wrong Airport" is aimed to inspire people who are victims of racism in corporate to speak up and raise their concerns; to encourage honest conversations with corporates to increase their efforts in embracing diversity and eradicating racism in their organizations. It also aims to serve as a compass to guide those people of all races who wish to be catalysts for change as we strive to develop a future economy built on strong moral fibre and the broader responsibility for a healthy, and productive society.

01

PREPARING FOR THE JOURNEY

As flight VS450 touched down in Atlanta, Georgia (USA), this was two weeks before I started penning down this book, I was overwhelmed by this feeling of joy, a powerful feeling of contentment and completion. Completion in a sense that I realized that it was time for me to be one of the global recipients of a highly renowned humanitarian accolade, one of the greatest moments in my life. This was the final check on the vision board that I had created with great deliberation and care many moons ago.

I was engulfed by gratitude and the feeling of being highly favoured by the Almighty. I chuckled as I heard the voice of one of my friends in my mind's eye. She always joked that she suspected that I was one of God's favourite children because I seemed to have it all. In my mind I was always relieved that she used the word "seemed" because, I have had my own fair share of challenges in this world with the difference being that God has indeed blessed me with a character that has enabled me to bounce back and to rise whenever I fall.

This accolade that I was to be honoured with in the USA was particularly close to my heart, given that the recognition bears testimony to who my parents were, and what values they inculcated in us as children to serve whilst prospering, to impact and move humanity using the gifts, talents, and skills that God has blessed us with.

I, the daughter of the Most High, am a humanitarian, proud to serve others. If it means baring my all and sharing my struggles with others who need guidance and hope, I do.

This is my destiny, or should I say my "destination" because we all know life has detours, unprecedented peaks, and troughs. Life can take you into different types of temporary detours where you would be certain that you have arrived at your intended destination, only to realise that it was another stop. These detours and stops have important lessons to be learnt and they grant us an opportunity to gather all sorts of insights and experiences that serve us well in our future endeavours. The profound insights we gain open our minds to great possibilities and help us navigate these detours of life. This is instrumental in building character for the "perfect landing" at the next destination, hopefully at the "right" airport, and to be able to be victorious and use the opportunities, the lessons learnt at the "wrong airport", to prepare for the next enriching challenge in this journey called LIFE.

Landing in Atlanta for the intended purpose of receiving what was a lifetime achievement was an unexpected reality in my life, that made me reflect on how far I had come. The question arises: "Was I prepared for my journey? Are we ever adequately prepared?"

A SOLID FOUNDATION

I have given a lot of thought to the significant experiences, the occasions in my life and of the people who shaped who I am today, such as my late mom.

My mother was an inspiration and a humanitarian herself. She started her career as a nursing sister working in the community at a local hospital; however, her calling became evident very early on based on the stories shared by her friends and family. She played multiple roles in the community such as nurse, "psychologist", community activist and sometimes intervened in family conflicts which involved women being beaten up by their partners, to the dismay of my father and us as kids. She was always available to serve.

From a child who was wounded from playing "helicopter" pretending to fly from the roof of a shed; to a pregnant woman about to give birth, she was ready to take on the duty of a caregiver. She worked "24/7" with such poise and patience. Over and above this, she made our humble family home a shelter for the destitute. My mother had an open-door policy to anyone in need. We always seemed to have one or two destitute people staying with us, and we shared what little we had with them, even our clothes. I remember that there was a gentleman who stayed in the "mjondolo" (shack) at the back. of our yard, and he had the most unpleasant body odour, which was persistent even after my mom tried donating some groceries that included toiletries to him. He used to love to come through to greet my mom inside the house and she let him in, with no judgement. She let him sit down in our lounge suite and asked us to serve him some cool drink on hot days. He was treated like any of her guests. The standing joke was that as soon as he left the lounge, we as kids ran to the cupboard so that we could "save" my mom who was probably struggling to breathe by then. The fastest one would grab the

"Airoma" (an air freshener) to spray all over the room and her response was always the same. She was more concerned about protecting his dignity, ensuring that he didn't see the fracas that we were up to, so that he wouldn't be offended. My mother respected and loved people.

I have a vision of her at the age of 70 living in the rural town of Mount Frere, giving talks to patients at a local medical practice and hosting Wednesday women's prayer meetings, which included a gym session. She was, in fact, the original "gym instructor" in the family.

I thought about all those great things that my mom infused into my soul by modelling this lifestyle of humanitarianism, and this reminded me of the wisdom that is Mother Teresa and what she once said: "Don't look for big things, just do small things with great love, the smaller the thing, the greater must be our love." I realized that my mom's small acts meant a lot in the community that she served and were the best preparation that I needed for my journey.

I would be myopic in my spirit if I do not also talk about my father, a local football official, who had a massive influence in the lives of young men in the area that we lived in and indeed my life. He was the manager of a soccer team called "Standard Football Club" based in Pietermaritzburg. This club became renowned as a talent pool for breeding up and coming soccer stars, feeding into national premium league clubs.

My father spent a lot of time with these young men, grooming them, not only for becoming great at their craft of football, but also in their lives holistically. What did that mean for me? It meant I witnessed unconditional love, not only towards my mother and us his children, but also extended to these young men, some of whom came from troubled families.

He was very humble in his quest to empower them with all the life skills he could possibly share, all this without judging them even when they were out of line. He took these moments as an opportunity to show love by coaching and spending more time with those that were troubled. Quite often these were the ones that would spend more time at our home. I could see that his soccer team cherished him dearly and so did we. All these experiences were valuable in giving me grounding and strength of character that would serve me well in the coming years.

I would be careless if I didn't talk about the women and men from my community who helped to raise me. Women in my community gave me the first glance of what it means to be an entrepreneur. What some of them managed to accomplish with limited education, was astounding to the onlooker. Their rewards were different to what is deemed as success today. For them success was seen and realized through the fate of their children with education at the forefront of every sacrifice they made. It wasn't about having the latest car or designer bag; it was about their children. I remember how as a child travelling on the bus, I witnessed scenes of them being chased out of town for selling fruit and vegetables on the sidewalk, which was illegal back then. Through it all, they kept on bouncing back. It is through their resilience, strong work ethic and discipline that my "kasi" became a breeding ground for a host of successful entrepreneurs and professionals.

My grounding as a child came from a solid foundation, one that could be shaken occasionally, but was never broken. These are the reflections that flashed through my mind as I touched down and walked through Hartsfield Jackson Atlanta International Airport, Georgia.

After the bustle of going through all the checks and verifications that allowed me to cross over into the USA (which ironically could represent the processes that we go through in our careers when we move to new institutions), I had time to think a little deeper about my career, my journey. As I waited patiently at the airport for my transport, I realized that this was a reconciliation of the key elements, the people and the experiences that prepared me for my journey, an eventful career that spanned over 25 years.

THE "BRICKS AND MORTAR"

I've had an outstanding career despite the challenges I have faced, and as I spent more time at this dream destination, I thought specifically about the times in my career that brought me to where I was, at that very moment. I immediately realized that having been in the corporate world in some of the most toxic environments and still being able to rise, meant that I was resilient. This was confirmed and narrated by current and former employees of some of organizations that I had worked at. Corporate, akin to humanitarianism, requires resilience. That is the big question, of where this spirit of resilience comes from given that this book "Perfect Landing. Wrong Airport" is very much about the courage to speak out; and the courage to keep going in pursuit of your success, no matter the circumstances.

As clichéd as it may sound, we spend a lot of time trying to succeed in the corporate world, and as such our grounding is very crucial, it's a necessity for survival. This is especially so for black women who bear the "double cross" of being both, black and female and are constantly under a pressure cooker because of racism and toxic masculinity. Many companies are not living true to the values that are on paper in terms of diversity, inclusion, and equity, especially because these are not lived in truth by the leadership and as such they are not being injected into the soul of the business.

It is rather unfortunate that I have personally experienced this first-hand for a long period of time directly or indirectly.

The fact that I have had an excellent record in corporate for the most part did not protect me from being treated unfairly and

rejected in other occasions. With that being said, one could argue that my experiences were the greatest set up for the strong, resilient woman that I have become. A woman who is now able to share and hopefully help others manoeuvre and navigate their journeys for the benefit of others.

Whilst the stories to be told in the "airports", the career destinations that I have landed at are sometimes lined with grim memories, it is fair to state that there were pockets of goodness to share that firmed up my grounding. Now part of this grounding I must declare, came from my initial exposure to the work force. I am forever grateful for my stint in the military. The relevance of me thinking about my military experience is that I have a photo of me standing in front of a military helicopter, that I peek at now and again on my phone. I often recall that I was at an air-force base with fellow troopers at one time, excited at the prospect of our first helicopter ride. I vividly remember my state of mind back then. You see, military training is tough, no matter your function. It is not only about the physical "bootcamp" program that is often shown in the movies, but most importantly a mental challenge. The extreme challenge and opportunity to rewire your mind for the ultimate battle on the battlefield and in life, upskilling one in strategy for war and to protect the lives of others as we prepare to go to war to protect our country and its people. It's not only taxing physically and mentally but also spiritually, because it tests one's willingness to move forward beyond logic, over and above one's physical capabilities. It becomes a spiritual battle where good conquers evil.

When I looked at the photo again, I realized that I had been through so much in the military, though not in vain. The truth is that the military is not for the faint hearted. What could have broken my will as a person, was in fact instrumental in building my character in terms of resilience, discipline and courage. The military took these traits to another level. At the time what was amazing was that I won the "Best Student" award during a very tough formative course in the early years of our military training. This was for many reasons, as narrated by the Sergeant Major leading the course at that time, including high grades in theory; overall leadership skills; resilience and generally living the core values of the military. This became a useful tool in my career as a leader going forward because in the military, whilst the common thinking is around attack, there is an emphasis on protection, protecting our country and the citizens. Again, I find alignment and synergy here with the experiences that were to follow in the corporate environment, which were about protecting and preserving self, being courageous and serving others through calling out the injustices that prevailed whilst risking becoming victimized.

MILITARY PRECISION

Those who have paid close attention to the military know that it is an environment that is very organized and structured to instil discipline within every member. This is an environment with very high moral standards, at least this was the case in my time. Back then, in the 1990's this included one's appearance in uniform, as well as the way that you showed up, whether in private or in public mattered. The way you presented yourself, even in terms of behaviour, was seen as a representation of the military wherever you went. It was of utmost importance never to allow your appearance to be the focus to such an extent that it would serve as a distraction for the task at hand. As an example, whilst there was a strong focus on neatness (overall cleanliness and hygiene) one would never see a soldier in military gear heavily "made up" and donning long colourful nails. The hair would have to be neatly styled in a simple cut or tied back. The rules were precise and stringent with the consequences of infringement being the discipline that was formally discharged the military way. The quest for excellence was non-negotiable. Members were kept on the "straight and narrow". This served as a lifelong habit, ushering in valuable lessons that put me in good stead as I landed and my corporate life unfolded.

There are endless stories that I could tell of how the military is a character-building institution. I learnt so much, including the importance of routine which was meant to train us to be consistent and precise in all that we do. I learnt the power of resilience and grit during those difficult times, when we were expected to go out into the cold and walk uphill to begin the day. We were then given limited time to prepare ourselves for a morning parade conducted in the freezing cold, a form of inspection to ensure that we presented ourselves immaculately and that our living quarters (military tents) were clean. Getting ready for the drill was part of the routine and I am proud to say that at some point I became a flag bearer. I need to point out that this is historically regarded as a very important task in the military, as one was carrying a symbol of what one is protecting, your country and its people. You're trusted to not only remember the drill but to also exude positivity whilst you're at it since you carry the pride and joy of your country, one which you would never abandon for any reason and defend to your death in a real-life war zone. This is the mindset of a true soldier.

EXCELLENCE PERSONIFIED: A GOD FEARING "STAR" LIEUTENANT

The question to ponder is, what was in it for me, in so simple a task of merely carrying the flag for a military squad at a training camp. Someone else might be tempted to view the stakes as low, benefits non-existent. Not this soldier! I have always understood the importance of elevating your performance, to drive everything you do with passion, even when the stakes are perceived to be low, a trait which has carried me throughout my career.

What does it take to be the best in class? This is the question that may have cropped up as I stepped up to accept the trophy; medal and gift presented to me as the Best Student in the military officers training course. Right there was the lesson, taking even the smallest task allocated seriously and celebrating all achievements no matter how small they may seem! This accolade certainly gained me a lot of respect in the military world; however, what is important for me is that it helped to strengthen my foundation, building my character to the next level. I appreciated those accolades and learnings because apart from being very inspirational, they also gained me long term respect as an officer from the highest office in the South African military, with further acknowledgement from the future Surgeon General who became a key support system in my career. I am humbled to say that to this day there are many fellow military veterans who have continuously connected with me to show appreciation for the inspiration stemming from following my journey and I have also equally been inspired by some of them. There are a few who have reached out several times for advice, trusting me (I believe) because of the kind of work ethic and resilience that they witnessed during my tenure in the military and beyond. I once received a note (an instant text message) from Sthandiwe Kgoroge, a former fellow university student who is a renowned South African actress and entertainer:

"Ella!!! I hope you still remember me from campus?
I hope you haven't lost your feistiness and political drive!
I admired you so much for just knowing your story at
such a young age! You haven't changed a bit, still
beautiful. Stay blessed! Sthandiwe."

This note reminded me of who I am and woke the "beast" in me, reminding me of the courage I once exhibited at university.

These are the types of calls that have continued to motivate me and to give me the courage to face the challenges presented in my career. As an example, a former fellow military officer recently called me to ask me to present at her organization's national workshop at their Head Office, citing that this task was too intricate to allocate to just anyone, and for that reason she needed to choose someone that she could trust, someone with integrity.

I must admit, I loved being in the military. I can recall that for several years whilst in corporate, I thought about going back quite often and went as far as making the necessary enquiries. With that being said, I knew that for me to be able to follow my dreams, I needed to move out and move on. To be honest, the remuneration was better, working conditions were more conducive, and flexible for a young mom in a multinational giant.

This was also enticing to me because I love to travel and to meet new people, whilst locking me into one space or a "thing" is potentially a spirit killer for me. Strange as it may sound, airports are like home to me. There's a mysterious thrill that I experience in that environment. Unsurprisingly, I experienced the same rush as I landed in Atlanta, it's a thrill of moving like a nomad from one place to another that fascinates and excites me.

I have always been convinced that my career moves are heavily influenced by God's flow, which brings me to the most important influence and anchor that has kept me going through the years, my faith in God. There have been several times when I have shown courage beyond my own expectations in corporate, and instances where I have taken a "Leap of Faith" away from what I have deemed as toxic.

Akin to my moves from one job to another, mainly because staying in a place where I could no longer serve others or that no longer served me especially in terms of my growth, did not cut it for me. Upon landing on a job, it's always very important for me to add value and to receive the support that I need to evolve and when this is lacking with no hope, it becomes quite clear to me that it is time to pack up and book the next ticket out. The common theme in my career or journey, travelling from one place to another on the flight is that with every landing at a job, with every destination, God had a task far bigger than my actual functional role.

Someone once asked me in an interview for a senior role: "What is your Superpower?" and without an ounce of doubt or flinching, my answer – PEOPLE. I love people, and as such motivating and influencing people becomes effortless. I thrive off connections with people and strive to make the lives of others better even in the workplace, as cheesy as that may sound. I thrive off the energy of others, and generally believe that we soak in and prosper from each other's energy and should aim to keep it positive. It is Winston Churchill who said: "United we stand. Divided we fall". That is the worldly view, which is amplified by the fact that I do believe that it is my trust in "God's flow" which strengthens me. God's love is what has been the compass and anchor that has kept me thriving in abundance.

This has been largely built by my unwavering trust in Him enabling me to unite and impact others for the better.

A CONTRADICTING LESSON

Unity or camaraderie is a key success factor in the military and yet it has been a base for some questionable characters, one of which I happened to come across in my career. The racist specialist doctor that I had the task to work with, albeit a very short period, was known for his notorious racist antics during apartheid and was allegedly responsible for permanently silencing many anti-apartheid cadres.

Even though I was not part of his direct cross functional medical team, one of my white colleagues was a member of his team, which is what he unapologetically preferred. I remember the week that my colleague was on vacation, and I was asked to stand in for her. I think I might have lost a kilo or two that week. I was terrified!

Experiencing him first-hand was a ruthless awakening to the fact that "hard core" racism still existed in the freshly unveiled new political dispensation. He had absolutely no qualms about showing how he felt about non-whites and at the time, I remember thinking that I was indeed better off on the professional side than being a non-white patient. On the night before the first ward round with this man leading the team, I was absolutely paralyzed with fear. I understood his 'modus operandi'. His was not just a "slap-on-the-wrist" type of act, it was carefully orchestrated to cause brutal destruction of the mind, denting one's self-esteem and hindering the ability to perform at one's peak. He was deliberate in killing one's core, stripping this one cell at a time. To make matters worse, I was standing in for a colleague who was regarded as one of the best in this specialization, a well experienced, high performing soldier who was used to working in highly pressurized conditions with difficult personalities that discriminated by race and gender. This was going to be a mammoth task made worse by the arrogance of a white man in a top-ranking military position who deemed himself fit to be a demigod, with the ability to save and take the lives of those that he deemed unworthy - "people of colour". This night I imagined myself having to face such brutality and racism, which left me sick to the pits of my stomach. Nevertheless, although my first encounter was something out of a drama series, with a little prayer and some grit, I survived the week in one piece.

The good news is that after some time, the news of this leader's racist antics (past and present) was revealed, which justified our fears. I remember watching the news and being in absolute shock at the amount of hatred that one human being could mete out to a group of innocent people by virtue of the colour of their skin. Little did I know that I would also experience this in corporate in varying degrees albeit not to the same extreme as his. I just remember saying a silent prayer before and during my first ward round, shaking profusely and praying that he wouldn't even look my way, let alone ask me any questions. Thank goodness that he didn't engage me, otherwise I would've probably frozen and looked the fool. With the next ward round it was much better because I knew the drill and was better prepared. When he eventually addressed me, I was well prepared. He had a way of lifting his nose up when addressing "people of colour" which showed his disapproval, a sight that I cannot erase from my mind and which I imagine now and again when encountering a racist in another era and area of my journey.

My deduction from all of this was that racists and bullies thrive from humiliating the other individual especially because of their lack of trust in their own capabilities, and just the lack of empathy and willingness to learn about and from other races.

What helped me to survive during this time, which I took with me throughout my career, was the power of knowledge that helped me become more confident and this, I believe, kept me safe from his wrath. Another tactic I adopted was being always on top of my game. I took time to understand the cases we were to discuss, getting into their depth and mastering my role.

My faith in Christ also built my confidence and made for a solid foundation, which was a key ingredient as I navigated my journey.

LOVE HAS NO COLOUR

As I continued my tenure in the military, I realized that I had a special bond with most of my patients who were Afrikaners. I could tell that they did not trust me initially; however, with time I managed to win them over by learning their language, showing them love and performing beyond mine and their expectations. I managed to face my fears and stand tall amongst those who intimidated me. I learnt how to use facts to defend my case. My stellar track record of consistent performance and knowledge also gained me their trust.

Whilst I had experienced racism as a young girl and later at university, this was my first encounter with "hard core" racism in the workplace. What was quite ironic was that through resilience and my survival strategy at the face of terror, potential and former perpetrators came round. At some point I ended up being the staff member who always received gifts from patients for being instrumental in assisting them to get back to a healthier version of themselves. I am not by any means a magician that makes racists repent, nor am I a saint; however, I do believe in the power of Love. I was just a black woman who respected those who had grown up with a specific view of all people, a woman who cared enough to meet those I didn't know well halfway and to learn a language for better connections and went above and beyond the call of duty to get them healthy as I did with any other patient. For them this was enough, but sadly for most racists I encountered in corporate this was NEVER enough.

As you come along with me on this "flight" that is my journey from destination to destination, I am quite certain that you will pick up the golden nuggets that kept me going and gave me the will to succeed, even during a depressed state. You will detect several survival cues in between the lines. The fact remains that good or bad, tough, or easy, supportive or challenging, great or small, directly or indirectly one has to inherently take all learnings with gratitude in the knowledge that it all comes together to build ones' character.

02

MY FELLOW
TRAVELLERS

No one traveller can ever say that they connected with each traveller that they've met along the way, as they ventured on about their own journey. Travellers may go to the same destination at the same time; however, their goals may differ. With that being said, the behaviour, attitudes and actions of fellow travellers may impact others. The travellers in this book refer to some of my former colleagues and leaders whom I have selected to represent using the interesting character traits I saw in the people I have met throughout my journey. These are the characters that had an impact on my career and that I believe influenced my journey as I conquered the obstacles that I encountered.

A learned friend of mine once briefly shared her learnings from a book that she read, where the concept of 'like attracts like' is unpacked. She narrated how the author writes about the law of attraction in relationships - that dysfunctional people attract dysfunctional people, and healthy people attract healthy people. It is fascinating how this happens, especially in long term relationships. There is apparently no scientific way to explain this type of work in the sphere of energy. The belief is that people are drawn to each other's energies and even though there is currently no metre to measure this attraction, there is enough to draw deductions from observations of the personalities that are to be described. The distinction is purely on observation, intuition, and the law of attraction. As uncomfortable as it is, one recognizes some of these traits because they exist within us and it is merely because of our values and belief systems, amongst other factors, that enable us to manage this for good or bad.

With every one of us being God's unique creation it would be near impossible to describe each of my fellow travellers individually with precision; however, the study of psychology enables us to define characters based on a group of traits and behaviours which enables us to understand personality types better. Although I have studied psychology as a module in various courses, I cannot claim to be a psychologist or an expert in this field and as such I have found my way to describe the main characters that have had an impact on my journey, good or bad. As a disclaimer, it is important to note that these are framed based on my personal experiences, observations and perceptions through capturing the common traits displayed by a variety of individuals in the different settings. In the last part of *Matthew 12: 33* (GNT) the Bible says:

"A tree is known by the kind of fruit it bears".

This scripture clearly illustrates the correlation between people and their backgrounds, giving us a glimpse into where they come from, and how this influences their behaviour, thought process, their soul, and the way they articulate their thoughts to us - this culminating in the good, the bad and the ugly. We get to see who people really are based on the background that carves their character trait. This is what birthed the main characters manning the key positions in the "airports" and at my career destinations.

THE GOOD

THE EAGLE

So much can be said about the character of the powerful eagle which is often referred to as the "King of the Skies". Whilst feared by many potential prey, it is revered by human-kind and is often referred to for its strategic and operational prowess. Whilst my journey is fraught with the evil racist characters who made my corporate journey almost unbearable at some point, I feel it necessary to introduce you to the Eagle who was more than a hero and a mentor, at times a saviour that brought hope in otherwise dire circumstances. Who is the Eagle and what is so special about him or her?

Those who observe eagles will tell you how sharp their eyesight is and once they have their eyes on the prize they swoop down and focus intently until they capture their prey. They are courageous and will not concede even in the most dangerous of situations. A scenario that comes to mind is how they conquer the snake, how they swoop the snake from its natural habitat taking them to unfamiliar, uncomfortable territory where they become vulnerable for the kill. Whether it's a snake or a mouse the treatment is the same. On the other hand, they have all the time in the world to nurture and train their young, releasing them to fend for themselves in an immature state only to save them when danger lurks. In corporate this character is a true leader that is fearless, goal-oriented and can be trusted with change management. They adapt and grow with their people and lead by example. They strive to create an environment where employees can grow to their full potential. They may seem ruthless in business; however, when it comes to people management, leading their own teams, they show humanity and fairness. They don't see colour like the racist does. Who would think that the Eagle would be a place of refuge for an emotionally wounded team member, beaten down by the discrimination of the past?

Whilst they would not appreciate weakness, the Eagle visibly defies the norm and gives confidence to those unjustly treated whilst dealing with those vicious characters who spit venom at the sight of the "clever black". They are willing to sit you down and articulate the game plan with such clarity of thought that inspires you to get up and give it your all. My Eagles came from all race groups, representing the diversity that is South Africa, illustrating once again what I believe about racism, that whilst this could be infused in a process of indoctrination, continuing with this atrocity during and after enlightenment is a choice. These strong leaders who were instrumental in making my corporate world fair ground in their sphere of influence, made it possible for me to conquer my fears and to thrive amidst the challenges.

THE BAD

TEACHER'S PET

This character is normally someone who has served the company for a long time and has been favoured by leadership. They are used to their prime spot in the company, then here you are, you've been brought in by the business with the expectation that you will help accelerate and take the business to the next level. You've been head hunted and handpicked from dozens of potential candidates and deemed fit for the role.

I equate the process to the many screening processes that one normally goes through to qualify for an entry visa in most countries, quite a laborious process, meaning that once one has been approved and received this visa, they fulfil all that is necessary to be at that destination, to be in that organization. This is not how the Teacher's Pet views the appointment of a strong black woman.

As an example, I was once roped in by a company that needed someone with experience in the mass market to complement their experience in offering premium and very niche products, predominantly targeted at white women. I walked into a situation where the Teacher's Pet immediately felt threatened by my appointment. This was a white woman reporting to another, who was outvoted during my appointment. She was now my new boss, begrudgingly so. Apparently, she was threatened by my credentials, and I could tell during the interview that my potential new boss seemed uncomfortable. After successfully landing the position, I walked into a situation where there was already some form of resentment, favouritism and loyalty built over the years between the boss and the Teacher's Pet, with a history of grooming and promoting the Teacher's Pet swiftly up the ranks.

For them you're an intruder who has basically moved into their territory. Their instinct is not to swoop at you from the onset; their behaviour is very similar to that of a Snake (which I expand on later) in that they will circle you with the main objective being to benefit from your specialist skills in a similar manner to leeches set to suck what they can and to disempower you.

Because most of the time one seeks to see the good in others, it's not very easy to identify that you're a target of their strategy of destruction. The Teacher's Pets that I have encountered have always given me nicknames or pet names (ironically) that have a connotation to a sisterhood, which immediately leads to one dropping their guard and becoming more vulnerable. This is the extent that they will go to great lengths in showing you how much they care for you. The aim of a Teacher's Pet is to blind you to their real intentions of blocking you from being seen or from "stealing" their position of being an executive favourite.

You on the other hand are innocently present to perform to the best of your abilities without knowing that you're in some sort of competition for the attention of the executives. It is obviously natural to expect that a new employee is out to prove their worth; however, in this instance your every move is watched like a hawk with ill intentions. The Teacher's Pet will do whatever they can to dim your light. Because they're very close to the boss and may have you as a joint enemy (as it was in my case), they're often one step ahead and are often briefed of divisional tasks well before you are. They're often your equal and as such you report to the same line manager; however, because you may be that "clever black" that's been brought in to change the game or you are just brilliant at what you do, they gang up against you to discredit you. How evil and hateful must one be to throw you into a key meeting with a brief that is completely incorrect just to prove what an idiot you are?! These are just some of the antiques of the Teacher's Pet.

What pops into my mind when I think of the Teacher's Pet is the smirk on their faces when they witness first your shock, then watch you stumbling at some point when you discover that you're off track. I have often wondered a few times what the conversations looked like behind the scenes and the type of mindset that someone must have for them to perpetrate the demise of an innocent equal. The sad reality is that they do not consider you as an equal at all and you'll find the tell-tale racial utterances and racist behaviour will begin to show up as time progresses. What they don't often realise is that while they call you a "sister", you're also there and you see how they refer to and think about black people in general when they let their guard down in rare moments. This is usually when your intuition should kick in and it becomes necessary to start devising a strategy for survival so that you thrive freely.

The Teacher's Pet will use their favourable position, their inside network and knowledge of the system to bring about your downfall. This certainly adds to the pressure that you set yourself to add value and can lead to the "beginning of the end" for one who is a victim on a downward spiral, making matters worse.

Another common trait of the Teacher's Pet is that they will amplify their efforts with every small victory or recognition that their victim celebrates. The more you overcome and get acknowledgement from the boss and others, the more they "tighten the screws". After my first successful campaign I remember witnessing the formation of a triad against me led by the Teacher's Pet. My initial joy was cut short by their actions where they were hell-bent on misleading me and amplifying my every mistake. Three white women on a mission to destroy this one black woman!

What is unfortunate is that your mistakes and how they are managed will not be the same as the Teacher's Pet. There was once a white guy who was an executive in sales who never used to visit customers as he should and would ration sales i.e.: 'fixing sales' such that his white salespeople always performed better than their non-white colleagues. It was a nightmare to watch with the white CEO, who was his best friend, just allowing this to happen. Even worse was that he was allegedly taking kickbacks from customers whilst black employees were always investigated for "suspicious" behaviour. Every time we roped in experienced black agencies, one was met with negativity. These characters were extremely averse to using black suppliers even though company policies were geared toward empowering brilliant black businesses.

Reporting such behaviour to the very same leader or to Human Resources (HR) becomes a frivolous exercise because these people are often close enough to have relationships outside of the office, at least in the instances that I have encountered in my career. I once discovered that the Teacher's Pet and the CEO had joint investments in businesses outside of the organization and even spent vacations in a jointly owned vacation apartment. HR acknowledged that this was not declared; however, no action was taken.

I remember that once my black colleagues trusted me enough, we would often talk about this unfair behaviour. Confiding in each other seemed to make the environment more bearable and to add a fun element. The Teacher's Pet would often be given a name such as the "Deputy", the "Vice" CEO and "Head Girl/Boy" because of what we witnessed i.e the leader often discussing key issues with him/her and making key decisions based on this. They were somewhat being given the power to act that way, showing bullying tendencies and giving instructions as if mandated by the leader. This bullying behaviour would happen in the presence of the leader who would not call them to order, giving them their ticket to becoming corporate bullies, with the main target being black employees. Rank or position did not matter, the colour of your skin determined how you're treated.

Another typical case in point was a white secretary who was ranked and compensated better than highly qualified black professionals in the business whilst being given fewer responsibilities. She often discriminated against black executives in terms of duties, was very disrespectful and was never reprimanded for insubordination when reported.

If you're someone like myself who stands up for herself, you will most certainly "amp" the Teacher's Pet up and it becomes an all-out war where you become a direct target. They will use every trick in their book to take charge of your fate wherever they can. What the Teacher's Pets are good at is playing the role of "Gate Keeper" when it comes to access to the boss, and this makes it even worse because some racist bosses will try to avoid dealing directly with you. They will either communicate with you on email to keep a record or through the Teacher's Pet so that they have witnesses. What also seems to apparently irk them the most is if you have a good command and annunciation of the English language, sounding brilliant. How dare you sound like, speak like and act like a white person with clout, like someone who knows it all? In my case the resentment was evident in those few joint meetings that we held as a team where I would come up with an idea only for the Teacher's Pet to be given the privilege to lead the project or worse still, for my idea to be rejected only to be reintroduced as her idea at a later stage. Despite your obvious superiority in experience and expertise, the scene is set for the Teacher's Pet to lead, to progress well beyond you in the organization, no matter what.

THE SNAKE

This character is very similar to the Teacher's Pet in some ways, even though the Snake might not be one hundred percent aligned to the boss per se. The Snake has similar characteristics because they would circle around you as if they are fond of you, when in essence, they are collecting facts about who you are and gathering "ammunition" that they can use to develop tactics to bring you down when the time is right. The Snake is a dangerous, ugly and devious character because you would not see their antics coming until it's too late, when they have wrapped themselves around you and are ready to crush you. They are basically what others refer to as "back-stabbers" since they would initially present themselves as your friend. They go above and beyond in offering you assistance, especially when you're newly appointed so that you become comfortable with them. They conduct thorough background research about you to the extent that it includes your personal life outside your working environment. These people will do anything to ensure that they have the upper hand so that you do not escape easily when they deem it necessary to bring you down. They will do whatever they feel is necessary to weaken your position.

If you've been in corporate long enough you would know that it is only natural that there is some sort of history around people out there, whether deemed good or bad. The Snake ensures that they investigate you to such an extent that they would go back to "dig" from your previous employers, they would troll you on social media and connect with your ex-colleagues, that they might know, in order to question them about you. The whole objective is to pull out the "skeletons from your closet" that they can use against you when they need to.

Why? I am sure that this is a question that might come to mind when thinking through all of this. Is this to prove what a consistently incapable incompetent undeserving black person you are? Is this yet another output of racism, jealousy and fear? Racists seemingly cannot fathom nor accept the possibility of being successfully led by a black person or being upstaged by one, let alone a black female. The Snake will not leave any stone unturned in order to gather information behind your back, with the ultimate motive of harming you. They lure you close so that they can slowly inject venom around your character to orchestrate your demise. As a successful black person walking through the doors of a corporate entity, where they believe you are a potential threat to their position, you unknowingly become instant prey.

These characters are really bad news especially given their sneaky slithery nature. They are hateful people who will catch you off guard with ammunition that they collect discreetly and will go on the offensive when your guard is down. Quite often their foremost tool is the use of the "power of the tongue" to tarnish your reputation. This is carried out whilst they breed complacency around you so that you blindly regard them as a friend. They're constantly close to you in order to gauge where you are at all times and to pounce when you're at your lowest or at your most naive state. At work we become vulnerable from time to time and veer towards the closest confidante. This is the most opportune time for the Snake to pounce!

In the meantime, often without your knowledge, they voluntarily become a stream of information to the business and others when it comes to matters relating to you. They would feed your colleagues and seniors with inaccurate information that would work to their benefit. Someone once sincerely asked me why it is that we fall for this trap time and again given that "we know that white people never loved us". We're all human, that was my answer, and it's difficult to gauge because not all are racist. One is often more inclined to trust and believe that people will acknowledge us for the human beings that we are.

What makes the Snake a more slithery character is that they are sharp and can pick up negative vibes from those of the same kinship in leadership positions, who become uneasy or threatened by your presence, and will feed into that. This is when they target already "fertile soil" by spreading false information amongst their fellow racists who delight at your demise. Inevitably the consistent flow of information, whether true or not, eventually impacts the perceptions the leaders and executives have of you.

The Snake is deliberate in his/her quest to destroy your reputation. They have mastered the art of 'stakeholder mapping', where they befriend people that matter most in your career progression. They are good at making suggestions around your state of mind, and driving false inferences regarding your capabilities with leadership. Their acts of sabotage are often counterproductive to one's efforts to upgrade and progress within the organization. The worst is that they act as the concerned friend, while secretly addressing your line manager directly, coming across as caring yet casting doubt on your character. What is often surprising is that in most instances your experienced black colleagues witness the Snake in action from the onset yet say nothing out of fear. The Snake is often well known in the company, prior to your on-boarding, for negatively impacting at least another person's career before your time, hence the fear that prevents colleagues from intervening or simply warning you. This person's motive is to seemingly guard against "black invasion". There's normally some track record around their behaviour with black people that may be eyebrow-raising and therefore it is important to take your time to connect with other people like you since they are likely to show you compassion and warn you once they feel that they can trust you.

Something else that we must note about the Snake is that often, they are imposters who want to hide the fact that they don't "know it all". Their insecurities are often exposed when they dilute the power of your education and experience with utterances such as: "You black people study too much" or "Degrees don't mean anything here". They seemingly have an inferiority complex, given that quite often they have "skeletons" that they desperately need to be locked in the closet. One can deduce that they act out of fear of being ousted by what they refer to as "clever blacks". The situation is made worse when your value is felt and there are signs of success at a portfolio that you work on, or you present innovative solutions. Racists just simply cannot withstand seeing a black person succeed and it is the very same with the Snake.

Ironically, it is most often during those times where you have overcome your challenges and start experiencing success that the Snake will emerge and show their true colours! We will discuss this in depth and how I dealt with such a character, in the latter part of the book.

In summary, the Snake character is out to lure you, inject venom in order to paralyze you, to devour you whole so that they can take charge of your career. This done so that they look better, getting you so frustrated so much so that you become despondent and incompetent, or just leave! This is a selfish, venomous and extremely dangerous character that can become very instrumental in destroying your career when they're let loose.

THE CHICKEN

The universally accepted slang meaning of the word "Chicken" refers to a spineless individual without the grit and courage to stand for what is right. What I have found in corporate is that most HR officers display this trait. They woefully lack the necessary skills required to support employees in distress due to racial discrimination. Our understanding is that HR people are best equipped with the knowledge to protect and foster fair treatment of all employees, no matter the level or the race.

In the beginning of my career, I was naive enough to rely heavily on them and was left puzzled, trying to figure out what it is that they or I was missing? Why would they be so vague and distant during times when they were needed the most? Why would they not stand up for the rights of employees even after consistent reports from various brave individuals? Was it a capability issue or lack of courage? The answer was revealed when I was privileged enough to meet one or two who defied the norms. It was simply a lack of courage and need for survival driven mainly by the fact that they didn't understand the law and feared their own demise. When one thinks of an HR person, you trust that they will serve both management and all employees fairly, that their mandate is for the wellbeing of all, under the factual guidance of the law.

Unfortunately, the "chicken-like" behaviour is destructive in its own way. In my encounters I learnt that confidentiality is a rarity with most of these characters and it will take very little for them to breach confidentiality to a racist Pitbull (which will be unpacked later) in a moment of weakness or when they feel the need to save their own skin. I would hazard a guess that they're also often in an unfair position, given that they often report to and are dependent on the very perpetrators of racism for their survival in corporate. As change agents, how do they then go back to their masters (who may also be perpetrators) to resolve complaints laid by employees, to resolve a serious and very uncomfortable issue such as racism? My answer to this is that it takes a very special kind of person to be an authentic HR professional. One that is courageous enough to carry out the basics of protecting the human rights of all employees whilst ensuring that the values of respectable corporates are enforced. In this book the "Chicken" is that HR person whose behaviour is to the contrary.

During my years in corporate I have seen the Chicken use their power to enable the Pitbull, in exchange for protection, validation and survival. They expose the employee to further victimization through immature behaviour such as sharing sensitive information with the racist! To appease the racist, they would sometimes find ways of assisting the Pitbull to "squeeze" the victim out of the system. I am quite sure that in this state of mind the Chicken barely thinks about the extended families that are affected when they pressurize people to the extent that they leave without jobs. The broader ripple effect of racism in corporate (to the extended family) is seemingly not considered here.

In fact, they often co-sign to psychological abuse that is immeasurable. What is sad is that the victimized employee may find it difficult to move on due to the untreated trauma of racism that could have been managed with the help of HR. What is also interesting is that the "domino-effect" can unfold in different ways where the victim either mimics the Pitbull in their own interactions with others down the line in order to survive, or they wither down and regress in terms of capabilities. Both are unfortunate given the role that the Chicken can play to curb this. On a few occasions I have asked respected HR people a few questions in the bid to change the status quo. Why does it seem as though some HR people are (to a certain extent) enablers of racism in corporate? I have often wondered at the basic criteria and personality traits that determine what a suitable HR professional in corporate should be, and that is one that would not be a "push over" that would be bullied by a Pitbull.

I was rather shocked when my younger colleagues at an entity that I worked for started calling the HR Director an "Ice Boy". They laughed at me (of course) when I wrote this term down initially and asked them what it meant.

When I related this information to one of the HR Managers, she was flabbergasted. Whilst she was aware of the negative perceptions around HR, she didn't realize that "it was this bad". I discovered that this is a word in South African slang that is used to refer to that friend in the group with the least power (often broke) who, in a social setting, is sent around, following orders from their group of friends for tasks.

The good news is that as my journey unfolded I was privileged to meet the brave ones, who made a major impact on my career.

THE UGLY

THE PITBULL

This is the worst of the worst, straight up, the racist bully and the most dangerous. This type of character is usually not involved in your acquisition into the company. Secondly, they often feel very threatened by your entry into the organization as an educated, articulate black person and their mission from day 1 is to prove that recruiting you into the organization was a grave mistake. They often carry the dual threat of being bullies as well as racists with their actions geared toward making you look like an incompetent black person, to frustrate you enough to drive you out of the organization or get you fired! They are there not to just "maim" your career but to "kill" it!

Racist bullies are often visible from the onset; however, because one is vulnerable in the beginning of a tenure one tends to ignore the signs or is reluctant to report the red flags, given that they are often subtle. The Pitbull often holds a certain degree of power which they try to use to show the business that you know nothing and that whatever you produce is only because of their intervention. They want to see you struggle so that they can be the hero who saves you in your disorganized, incompetent state. It's really all about them! Quite often they have been with the organization for a while and have the relationships and information that can make your transition into the business a little easier or harder. In a weird kind of way, they visibly want to be seen as your coach or mentor and then take the credit for all that you bring to the table as a black person. Like the Snake and the Teacher's Pet, the resentment becomes quite evident when it seems as though you come with superior knowledge. The difference with the Pitbull is the level of aggression and danger that they present. What they really want is for you to struggle. They want you to come to them begging for help so that they can tell you what's wrong with the business and what the solutions are, which is counterproductive for a business looking for fresh thinking. Even though you have been brought in to bring about change and a fresh new perspective about the business; especially in categories that are consumed by black people, they hate the fact that you are there. Now one could argue that this might be the behaviour meted out to newbies of all races; however, this has been blatant behaviour illustrated towards black people even in instances where new employees of all race groups are employed simultaneously. Black employees are simply singled out by racist Pitbulls.

The oddest element though is that deep down Pitbulls know your capabilities because they take the time to research you too. At some point when they need your expertise, they will source it using their position power, with the condition being that they will take the acknowledgement for themselves. They may then publicly attack you should you show any signs of claiming credit for your own work. It is during these times when strange behaviour ensues. They may acknowledge the reason for your existence, referring to the main reason for you coming on board to transform the business, and yet for most of your tenure, they act differently and will not allow you to become a prominent player through acts of sabotage.

They have no empathy at all and will abuse the power that they have to belittle you and break you down psychologically and spiritually, such that your confidence and output are affected. They withhold key information and humiliate at every chance given, even in front of your subordinates, external stakeholders, and colleagues in meetings. They minimize your powers by bulldozing your decisions, all this in attempts to make you feel and look incompetent. Although they have researched you, they often seem surprised at what you can accomplish despite their efforts. Quite often they may try to dilute your efforts, implying that you may have overstated your abilities. Like a real-life Pitbull, they simply will not let go until your demise is final. They are a very dangerous kind!

It is important to unpack this character further, given that they are at the forefront of influencing my experiences post landing at the various organizations in my career.

INTELLECTUAL THEFT

Let me take you through an example of when I had an experience with a Pitbull who somewhat acknowledged my capabilities when a category within a business needed a revival strategy. Being the one in charge and in the firing line from the board, the Pitbull became restless and changed her behaviour with one quest in mind; to complete the assignment and "save her skin". The setting for this incident could not have taken place in a place more beautiful than the picturesque Franschhoek, where my partner and I were guests of honour at the wedding of a prominent family member.

The A-listers in SA business, celebrities and government officials were present at this occasion, a never to be repeated opportunity to network with these personalities. This became tainted by my then racist Pitbull boss's insistence that I complete this recovery document over that weekend knowing my plans fully well in advance. I hardly slept a wink on the night before the wedding and I remember longingly watching my partner sleeping peacefully in the most beautiful hotel. There I was on the wedding day exhausted, with no proper makeup on nor a fancy hairstyle like all the other women. I simply wasn't at my best and felt so self-conscious when asked to stand up as a family member during the proceedings.

Nevertheless, I put together a sterling document and successfully sent it through to my then Pitbull boss, who (to my dismay) simply inserted a title page with her name and designation and submitted it as her own work without acknowledging my valuable input at all. Despite her antiques of trying to discredit me, the Pitbull took my intellectual property as is and went ahead taking full credit for it, something that she never did to her white subordinates.

I witnessed this as she would go to great lengths to make it known when my white counterpart submitted what she deemed as good work. In a very similar scenario, she ensured that she assisted my colleague to put the document into a presentation and secured a time slot with executives to ensure that she had her "time in the sun", in the spotlight to present the work to the leaders of the organization. This was quite painful to see in action. It was almost as though she didn't see me as a human being with feelings. This is the common factor that I have seen from Pitbulls. This type of character is ruthless and very mean. I often asked myself the same question, why do they hate black people so much? These people REALLY despise black people.

Seemingly, if it all was to go according to their wishes, we would be subservient beings in their world, just following instructions. What we are good for would be to exist more meaningfully just as consumers since black people are the majority in South Africa. Only our money is good enough! According to them we seemingly do not deserve to walk in the same corridors, in the same positions, being executives in corporate South Africa. Who are we to lead the narrative in any of these businesses? These racist Pitbulls do not seem to possess the moral compass to at least respect black people as human beings first.

In another organization I shared a game-changing innovation and product development idea that had the potential to take the business to another level, one that was rejected profusely only to have it assigned to my counterpart at a later date as a fresh new project. How do you report or reprimand the Pitbull in this instance given that they craft the intellectual theft in such a way that it appears as though it's a completely new idea that came forth during a brainstorming session or is disguised as an output of another process such as research? In this instance my sanity was saved by the research and development professional within the organization who approached me (albeit discreetly) to validate my thoughts. I've often called the Pitbull an evil mastermind for this reason. The sad part is that Pitbulls are able to operate this way for so long because they're not reprimanded successfully.

Apart from being in an infuriating situation it is demotivating and can be a major factor leading to severe depression because one tends to blame themself for not having the courage to fight back - without understanding the power of the Pitbull and the difficulty of proving their atrocities.

WEAPONIZING PUBLIC HUMILIATION

Some call it systematic racism, where an ideal environment is created within the organization for the growth and development of white people whilst in the same breathe this environment proves to be destructive and debilitating for blacks. This is the narrative of the Pitbull, indoctrinated by generations like him/her who made the apartheid government reign and thrive for a long time.

One of the tools is weaponizing public humiliation. The instances where this was displayed by the Pitbull are so many; however, what comes to mind first are some of the antics that would unexpectedly show up at key meetings that leave the victim feeling embarrassed and hurt. The Pitbull has no qualms at turning against you, displaying shocking behaviour that would discredit you despite the fact that you are all supposed to show up as a team. I think that one of the worst instances was when my then Pitbull boss made every move not to meet with me before a key meeting whilst assisting my white counterpart after hours (as I discovered later) to put together a presentation. Because we had not aligned prior, I was not aware of the required updates and of course she immediately deliberately distanced herself from my position during the meeting and made me look like a complete idiot. I remember putting up a specific slide and hearing her mutter as though I wasn't even present: "Oh no! This is incorrect; I don't know why she put that slide up?" ... as though I was an imbecile.

In some instances, we would align beforehand and yet she would still behave in the very same way, which made me realise that I was basically on my own and had to find means to survive, if I were to succeed. Instead of supporting and substantiating my facts she would either watch me being crucified by seniors from the cross-functional team or do the condemnation herself! This peculiar behaviour showed up consistently and was starkly absent during the presentation of my white counterparts.

FIGHT OR FLIGHT

Very often I (and some of my black colleagues) found ourselves at a crossroads - fight or flight? In most instances with this type of character, one finds themself walking on eggshells to avoid the backlash and brutality that follows through when confronting issues. The Pitbull initially displays passive aggressive behaviour that can escalate to public verbal attacks often in meetings - when the opportunity arises. Pitbulls are also very manipulative beings that would often befriend HR managers to ensure that they know what is happening. This behaviour is designed to keep abreast of any complaints from their subordinates so that they can be disregarded or "managed". My theory has been that they are aware that somehow, they are flouting labour laws, given the concerted effort they extend to cover their tracks with HR. In my experience they would be a few steps ahead so that by the time you decide to fight back by reporting to HR, they would have already cast doubt on your reputation with false information to taint your reputation and discredit you. This to avoid being taken to task based on SA Labour laws. When under attack from a Pitbull the question at the crossroads is always whether to fight or escape. The risk is that once the Pitbull is aware that you've reported them, they up their ante on their efforts to discredit you and you need to prepare for the mental onslaught that follows. This is a frightening thought especially for a young professional, because it is common knowledge that when a Pitbull grabs a hold of you, they don't let go and the result could be "fatal". This is strikingly similar with these characters in corporate. FACT - THEY HAVE NO MERCY!

South African labour laws should protect all employees from such unlawful practices; however, the interpretation and execution thereof are at the mercy of company executives, with the major role being that of HR practitioners. Over and above this South Africa has a BEE policy whereby one of the key elements is the integration of black people in the workplace, requiring a quota of black employees in management roles. Whilst these Pitbulls are often aware that they are potentially breaking the law, I do believe that they bank on the fact that it's not that easy for many employees to prove that these atrocities take place, with so many blurred lines and the lack of support from HR. Racism in corporate poses a potential reputational and financial risk; however, most businesses seem to be the playground for Pitbulls.

The question is: "How is this possible when the world is seemingly so "woke" about issues around racism and inequality in general?"

The tactics to avoid disciplinary or legal action seem to vary. These include but are not limited to manipulation and intimidation. I remember an instance when the Pitbull saw one of my black colleagues chatting to HR after which she called her into her office to remind her that she (the Pitbull) knew everything that was happening in the business and was well connected, meaning that she could impact her career negatively. This was a clear message that should she decide to go and report to anyone in the business, the Pitbull would find out and she would 'deal' with her, affecting the progress of her career. The victim, an intelligent black woman, resigned two weeks later and was relieved of her duties within 24 hours. Somehow the previous atrocities of the Pitbull were disregarded, and she was protected because the business allegedly "needed her more" than the victim. This is one of the ways that the Pitbull gets away with their horrid actions, unlike a CEO I once heard stating that he did not care how good the person was, he would get rid of any individual who discriminated against any other employee.

The "modus operandi" of the Pitbull is to blast the victim with threats that make it very difficult to take them on, especially when it is evident that they are "untouchable". They are in a position of power and can seemingly decide your fate. They often also play on the fact that many black men and women have extended families that they need to take care of and are often desperate to hold on to these jobs so much so that they would rather remain silent than report and risk losing their jobs. They're often stuck in a paralytic robotic depressive state that is neither "fight" nor "flight", but a plight for survival.

CORPORATE STUNTING

I've said many times that Pitbulls are agents of corporate stunting that can affect your corporate and personal growth as well as your life stability. Sadly, it is common to watch many vibrant black employees retreat and eventually lose their spark during their tenure in organizations where Pitbulls are allowed to thrive. Other than that, they would hop from one job to another to find peace, where they can thrive and add value without discrimination. That's when flight seems to be the best solution to protect themselves psychologically and to protect their reputation. It is a common practice for the Pitbull to use their power during reviews and to minimize the victim's contribution to the organization. Despite being the architect behind the success of some key brands in an organization, a Pitbull boss always found a way of reducing my scores during assessments under the guise that the scores were the same as his and he wouldn't be getting a bonus. I later accidently discovered, during a meeting with HR, that this was a blatant lie and that he was earning huge bonuses by "working the system".

The question is: "What happens when you report this behaviour, given that we all aspire to grow professionally?"

Here is an example of how the system can fail the employee, and in effect continue to contribute to stunting their growth.

In corporate, performance reviews are standard and are often complemented with personal development plans geared toward assisting in your growth as an employee. This is not confined to a specific level and would include a 360-degree feedback session. In this instance a few brave individuals managed to slip several complaints regarding the Pitbull into the suggestion box.

An HR professional from within the business, was deployed by the global team to intervene on the matter. Unfortunately, this did not yield any positive results since this intervention was done in the presence of the perpetrator, who took full control of the proceedings. The fact that he was allowed to be in the room, with a very intimidating demeanour, was shocking and brought the whole intervention into question. This became yet another opportunity for the Pitbull to showcase his power. He scrutinized all the points that were written about him on the board (via "post it" notes) in order to decipher whose handwriting it was that was attached to a point and later victimized the individuals. I was one of those 'victims' and it went to an extent that I was even attached to points that I had not written about, due to my outspoken nature during the session. A particular point which I am known to be vocal about and which made him visibly uneasy was around issues of favouritism and racial discrimination. This is the type of environment where an incompetent thieving white receptionist and executive secretary had more equity and power in the business than a brilliant, hardworking black executive. I had pointed that out several times after being disrespected and blatantly treated differently by this young white woman. It was clear that it was race, skin colour that mattered.

The stunting would happen systematically using internal processes and subtly in terms of attitudes and behaviour. Many unsuccessful attempts were made to tarnish my reputation to limit my remuneration and stunt my growth.

REPUTATIONAL DAMAGE

Being the worst of the fellow travellers, one of the questions when dealing with a Pitbull is around how you would really deal with this type of character in such a way that you get the credit that you deserve and thrive as a professional. We've established that no matter how much you deserve it, the racist Pitbull will never willingly allow your efforts to be fully recognized. Secondly, if you do not "suck up" or take on a submissive demeanour that is openly dependent on them to thrive, you become a target of the extreme end of racism. Thirdly, the quest to dilute your power and your brilliance becomes a mission, to the extent that it affects you financially and mentally.

The Pitbull will use their power to tarnish your reputation in forums that count for your progress, sharing untrue stories about your performance and often making you the scapegoat where there are issues. This would often happen in meetings where you are not present to state your case.

In this cycle of such passive and active brutality against your character, it is not uncommon for one to become demotivated and for the victim to begin to doubt themselves and their capabilities. One's mental state can be negatively impacted here, and, in some instances, depression is inevitable. When there is no channel to use as a trusted outlet or the channels that are present are blocked by threats and mistrust, serving only as a precursor for victimization, then the situation becomes worse.

"Gaslighting" is a common tactic that the Pitbull uses to

further deepen your thoughts of self-doubt and to plunge you into a submissive state, carefully crafted to render you ineffective and your soul destroyed.

In the upcoming chapters these characters are unpacked further, revealing the impact that they had on my career growth whilst highlighting the strategies I adopted in rebuilding myself towards the success I am experiencing today.

03

LOVE AND HATE

There's a song with the lyrics: "There's a thin line between love and hate" that was released by the R&B group H-Town in 1996. I resonate with the sentiment of these lyrics. It is indeed true that you can love someone to the extremities and give them your full complete love; however, a betrayal of some sort can lead to such extremities in the opposite end of the spectrum - hatred! There's an intense temptation to draw parallels with the words of this song, the emotional roller coaster experienced in relation to the white characters that I encountered in my career, those that tried to diffuse my light. The depths of these emotions are such that the hatred one can feel at some point can be toxic, especially when you're in a corner, a position where you feel as though you cannot do anything, engulfed by helplessness and fear, driven by the racism experienced.

The sad part is that this tends to completely overshadow the good, blinding you to acts of kindness whilst on the opposite spectrum, the random acts of kindness of others can turn the hatred into love and appreciation, really an oxymoron.

THE ONE YOU LOVE

At first glance one might believe that this book is about how much hate one harbours for white people because of the atrocities experienced in the past from the white Pitbull racists. Totally incorrect, hence the importance of this chapter of the book for me. In my career I have met the most amazing white "brothers and sisters" who have supported me during my darkest hours. I won't say "some of my friends are white" given the negative connotations behind this phrase, since the unofficial perception is that it is more likely to mean the opposite! Then, what do I say? How do I highlight and show my appreciation for those who were born on "enemy" ground but chose not to embody the hatred that is racism? How do I honour those who risked their own privileged positions at times, for human good? This chapter is an attempt at this, sharing my experiences with this group of individuals who showed genuine love against the backdrop of intensely racist settings.

The Zulu greeting "Sawubona", which means "I see you", is the best acknowledgement bestowed to anyone, so powerful in its symbolism as it shows the recipient that you see them, their core, including their spiritual make up and you acknowledge their worth. My unlikely friends were and remain amongst those who have treated me with the utmost respect and dignity, even when I was at my weakest and had nothing much to offer. Whilst it was much easier to treat me as a worthy professional during the times when the balance of power was in my favour, it is important to point out that these individuals personally treated me with utmost respect from the onset and have never wavered, to the extent that I have received some of the best character testimonials from them. Can you imagine confiding about the atrocities of a white person to another, without any backlash or judgment? Such are these friends. What was and remains most astonishing is the frankness and ability of those kind souls to articulate without fear, any instances when they deemed necessary to point out when they thought that I might be overreacting. This honesty was important to me so that my voice would not lose credibility because of frivolous unjustified complaints.

There were times where I would share my progress on various platforms on social media and I would receive a surprise call from them sharing what an inspiration I am to them as well, as they pursue their dreams. Because of the mistrust that has been sewn amongst the different race groups one may be tempted to ask the question: "How do you know that you're not being fooled, that you are not dealing with a "wolf dressed in sheep skin"? The answer lies in the Godly intuition that one is gifted with. In the most traumatic of times, they'll show up where they seemingly have nothing to gain from you. People like that are hard to come by. The ones who call when you're jobless in the middle of COVID-19 just to check if you're okay and to motivate you to keep going when times are tough. These are the genuine human beings who really care despite the racial differences.

Sometimes you might become confused especially if you grew up in an intensely segregated society like I did. Take for example the young white Afrikaner soldier who had a major crush on me during my days in the military. Young and fresh out of university, I could easily tell that he was a little confused. In between our training sessions the rest of the crew found pleasure in teasing him because of his obvious interest in me. I was also teased by the female troopers who often jokingly asked me what I had given to him, referring to love potions. Because I was a married woman back then, I didn't tell them nor did I show that I liked him too and would have probably married him if I was younger and he had asked. He was very smart and quite handsome as well. He also "worshipped" the ground I walked on and would ensure that I was okay, that I had enough to eat and that I was happy. I really loved his attributes as a caring human being.

Another experience with this love came from a woman who also defied the doctrines of her upbringing and showed genuine "Ubuntu" through respect and true appreciation for my brain. She would always relate that she felt that I was blessed to be educated and intelligent, something that she didn't have. She was very authentic about me as a human being first and in awe of what I have achieved as a black woman. I was her role model, she said once, as she told me how she admired the resilience in rising above barriers, the fact that the circumstances that I grew up under did not deter me from achieving my dreams. As she compared her circumstances to mine, I looked her in her eyes to check if these were the words being spat out by a Snake, this as she continued to relate how she had not managed to go as far as I did despite her privileges. She would trust me enough to guide and mentor her through any task that she couldn't manage and would openly acknowledge my input.

This was not the only case where I received kindness from her kinship, some of whom worked for external entities. Some of these women had worked for companies that serviced mine and were present for some of the most embarrassing moments in my career. I could see them cringe at some meetings where a racist Pitbull publicly humiliated me.

Strangely enough even though they would not gain much from a weakling like me they still followed me throughout my career to the point where they would still connect after relocating to different countries. For me, it was very easy to tell who was genuine and who was not. Sometimes the relationship started out as professional and then progressed to a meeting of the minds to the extent that we enjoyed conversations outside of work. We shared similar work ethics, values, principles and most importantly, our belief in God. I honestly love them for who they are because they kept me sane. They were consistently there for me as I battled on, cheering me on when I needed it and going to great lengths to ensure that I succeed. When times were tough, and I realized that I needed to move out of a toxic environment they would assist with the job search and serve as my reference.

In addition to the above, when I was a rep most of my customers were white women. Again, they looked more at what I had to offer versus the colour of my skin. This was so, to the extent that I received supplier awards because of these trailblazers who drove the industry and never compromised on the standards of quality and outputs. They recognized me for who I am. These are very learned academics with a wealth of experience. I received quite a number of these awards over the years which helped to keep me motivated and to strive to do better every time.

What about the black women who were in the trenches of corporate with me and who continue to support and pray for me, in the most challenging of settings. These strong, resilient queens have a special place in my heart, having played a very significant role in my journey, in who and what I have become. Our intertwined stories are best told in another journal of events …a journal of the warrior women in corporate.

THE "LOVE LANGUAGE"

When we unpack the "love language" of the Pitbull, Teacher's Pet and Snake we're referring to the overt depiction of love with ill intent. This is the first category, those that will show extreme love and kindness during instances where you share concerns around discrimination and then they act surprised when you report these acts of racism. In some instances, you're made to feel like a "cry baby" or that you may be hallucinating. This is seldom depicted by the Pitbull who is normally out to get the jugular from the onset. With all these characters, the sad truth is that you may discover at some point that they've known all along. They're in on the plot to your demise. As an example, I was astounded once when I overheard the boss saying to a Teacher's Pet that I had reported: "Listen, ease up a bit, she's already come to me to report you."

The second are those who will seek to befriend you and call you in endearing terms such as "Love"! Imagine the excitement with which I approached my partner once, gushing about someone who turned out to be a Snake. I remember my partner warning me: "They never loved us! How can you say that's your friend?" He did turn out to be partially correct I should think! It didn't take long for me to experience the harsh reality of betrayal from that very someone whom I genuinely regarded as my best friend at work. This was most evident when she was within her own circles where she would switch behaviour completely and the true colours would show - to my utter dismay.

So, what does this all mean? To me it meant that despite my anger at these characters, I needed to be careful not to paint a whole race group of individuals as Snakes, Teacher's Pets and Pitbulls. This meant that despite the awful journey that ensued and is yet to be unpacked in the chapters to follow, it is important to highlight that this is not about all white people. This is about a play on the emotions of love and hate in the game of racism amongst individuals who happen to be in this group and how delicate it is. This is about those that showed such racial hatred to the extent that they exercised psychological torture that left me and many others in a destructed mental state that needed courage and strong will to win the battle of the mind, contrasted by those who showed love.

What we can see here is that an output of racism (whether subtle or overt) is this wave of emotions that can be confusing at times, which can take a toll on one's mind and emotions. The people on the receiving end often end up showing signs of depression and erratic behaviour similar to that which landed a former colleague of mine in a mental institution. As much as it is not evident on the outside the mind is constantly debating and assessing whether this or that individual is a friend or foe. Are they genuine or are they a "wolf in sheep skin"? The mind is in constant overdrive because deep down you want to be certain and you don't want to be blinded by the facade of "real" racists. Once you've succeeded in making the distinction, it's a relief and supports the sentiment that stops one from making blanket assumptions about a race. This would be counterproductive in that one's energy could force these "good humans" to focus on defending themselves and proclaiming their innocence instead of showing love.

There are genuine acts of kindness that illustrate this love such as the "madams" who chose to house the kids of their helpers in their homes and send them to the best schools, the same as their own children. I remember a lady who even built a mansion for her helper in her rural village to ensure that she has a secure retirement. This was an unsolicited act of love.

This then calls for a deliberately sensitive approach versus the rot that still fills our boardrooms with hatred bred from racism. Am I hurt by the atrocities of the Pitbull? Absolutely! Do I hate a whole race group that nurtures my racist perpetrators? Most certainly not! As I unpack my journey, my landings and experiences in these various entities, the mixture of emotions will become evident. At the same time, you will see how God prevailed by showing unconditional love through those who chose not to see colour but to show love. God's love was illustrated through these individuals, and this gave me the will and guidance to determine boundaries.

"CUPID" IN CORPORATE

The option to speak out is the one only followed through by the brave given the offensive brutality that is evident when one speaks up against the racist Pitbull. How then does one deal with a Pitbull, given that they systematically exclude you from forums that include their superiors, so that you do not become comfortable enough to address the issues of racism directly beyond their level? With most HR personnel seemingly powerless in terms of dealing directly with racism in corporate, what are the options in dealing with a Pitbull? Often HR are aware of these malpractices with most failing to deal with them because of their own agenda for survival given the power that the Pitbull has.

In my experience, as previously mentioned, I have met one or two who have been vigilant in exposing such behaviours and are advocates for justice within the workplace. It is through these champions that one has been able to progress in corporate thus far. Whilst they are not publicly acknowledged and their opinions and work are often disregarded by leadership, they are the underground, background cheerleaders that keep most employees affected by racism optimistic and passionate. In this instance I regard them as the "Cupids" in corporate.

Together with these individuals it was possible to formulate a "survive and thrive" strategy which kept me motivated and productive.

04

A LIGHTER SHADE OF BLACK

Most people today know of the atrocities that came with apartheid where black South Africans were discriminated against politically and economically. The country was racially segregated with the white ruling minority enjoying the highest standard of living, compared to all the other race groups. Included amongst the discriminatory laws of the time was the Group Areas Act which came in effect during the 1950s. With this Act it meant that there would be clear segregation of business and residential areas which were further demarcated according to race groups. To accommodate white people, all other race groups were removed from prime residential areas and relocated to racially designated areas, with those classified as Coloured and Indian being granted better housing and financial assistance than those classified as Black.

The population registration act of 1950 required all

people in South Africa to be classified under a race group using a number of characteristics, with the colour of their skin as a major indicator, amongst others. The infamous "pencil test"/ "hair test" was also used in the early days of apartheid as a bizarre way for further classification amongst those who were not classified as white. All non-whites were regarded as inferior, which included Indian, Coloured (multiracial) and Black (African origin), whilst those regarded as Caucasian were classified as white - the "superior" race. This was based on the social acceptance of skin colour complimented by descent. There was harsh punishment for those who did not comply with these racist laws and were found to be in an "incorrect" area. The irony was that even with these laws in place, there was a rise of the multiracial group which clearly showed that there was forbidden interaction amongst the various race groups which was the "crime" highlighted in Trevor Noah's book called *Born A Crime.*

It was compulsory to be classified under a race group with the Department of Home Affairs for record keeping purposes; however, this also gave way for further discrimination, with those classified as Indian and Coloured being granted advantages that black Africans were deprived of. They were what is referred to in this book as the "lighter shade of black" that were privileged based on a social hierarchy which was created and used by the white minority to allocate resources such as housing, education, jobs, remuneration and more.

When my twin sister and I were born, we are told that our father ensured that we were classified as Coloured because of his ancestry so that we could be able to leverage the privileges that came with being "a lighter shade of black". Whilst we gained from this act in the sense of securing access to better resources in our formative years, this was limited because of our stronger African heritage (Xhosa and Zulu) and the fact that my parents opted for a lifestyle in the township, which influenced our cultural experience.

With that being said, to this day, I still believe that the exposure to the two "worlds" was enriching. The irony is that once one married into "the darkest shade", into a Zulu family, one seemed to be somewhat "relegated" to the least privileged, the "darkest shade", the most underprivileged disadvantaged group. The difference in the treatment was even more prominent at university and in the workplace.

At university there was systematic racism that affected the darkest shade, black students more, even up to the way that the timetable was set. In addition, some lecturers were so mean and displayed such public resentment toward black students to the extent of publicly humiliating us during lectures. This was my first taste of stark racism in a space where all races were allowed to be together, to study together and where the "other" races that were a lighter shade seemed to be treated better. I identified more with the disadvantaged group and as such I was also discriminated against more harshly.

PSYCHOLOGY OF A "BETTER" SHADE

A consequence of the unequal treatment of the predominantly darker skinned blacks, amongst non-whites, gave rise to the phenomenon which I have coined "A lighter shade of black", where the other groups where granted more privileges, treated better, with some consequently feeling superior to blacks because of the design of apartheid which somehow positioned them better than blacks. This would manifest in the way that some would ill-treat black people where they were in positions of power, or they would act as enablers and make the situation worse.

In the racist American era, they would probably have been

the "house slave", who often believed that they were better than all the other slaves. Whether we like it or not this continues in the corridors of corporate today where there is discrimination across the non-white "colour spectrum". So, the real question is and always has been: " What has the colour of my skin got to do with what I deserve as a human being? Why is lighter better? Does having a lighter skin mean that your brain works better? What does this mean for a highly qualified, experienced black professional with a stellar track record and capabilities, who is discriminated against by whites and non-whites with skin that is a lighter shade of black? The fight is amplified, it is made worse.

As I walked into some of these organizations, I walked into the foyer not only as a black woman who needs to prove her worth, but also as part of the human race that was at the bottom of the barrel. In my experience I have witnessed how some of the "higher order" non-whites have used this to their advantage to sadly bully black people in order to survive. In most instances they have leveraged on the weaknesses that are a consequence of a poor education system where some black people still struggle to articulate themselves. So, for some blacks it feels like one has walked into a storm or stepped into hot water. It's quite disheartening to make the discovery of a racist environment after being excited at the prospects of a new career move, made even worse by the betrayal from your brothers and sisters of a lighter shade. As you gain experience you look forward to adding value and your objective is to make a positive impact and to make your mark. Your good intentions become tainted because of the treatment you get from being "the darker shade of black".

Someone once warned me about an organization where this was rife stating that "the moment you are black here you start from the bottom", you must prove that you are a worthy human being. The starting premise is that you do not know much and you're not capable, which means you must build your way up.

With all your credentials and qualifications, you must still build your way up. It is almost like an empty corporate bank account or a credibility scale that requires you to start pouring in the minute you walk into the organization.

It's not that often that one finds a racist Pitbull that is "a lighter shade of black", however, I am sad to state that I have witnessed this in full swing. Given the powers by the global management of an organization that was of the same heritage as this Pitbull, she went into full steam bullying, which was made worse by stark racist moves. It was her strategic moves that enabled her to take the reins of the business using her common heritage with the global corporate office. At first, she systematically "cleaned" the system of all the "clever blacks" who posed a threat to her position of power. There was clear discrimination against blacks, with cases of sabotage and bullying that led to a mass exodus of black talent. An organization that truly cares about people should have "nipped" this behaviour "in the bud" from the onset because of the impact on people's lives which eventually impacts productivity and the business.

The sad truth is that black talent is often lured into these organizations under false pretences, for selfish reasons, in order to improve the company's BEE scorecard. They are misled into believing that they will be treated with basic respect, which is sadly not the case once they become settled, or even sooner than that. Most black people will relate when a new "victim" enters the organization, it's like watching the rerun of a movie, with the audience having an idea of what will happen next without having the power to stop it. That in itself is painful to watch.

In one of the cases I was actually also enticed into an organization under false pretences that would unknowingly down-grade my corporate stature, which actually shows how selfish this group of people can be. As a collective with similar struggles, one would expect that there would be comradery and we would take care of each other or be fair to each other, at the very least. The sad truth was that in this case I was brought in for very selfish reasons to be an ally in the battle for power. The Pitbull did not care about me and the impact that her moves had on my career. She was more concerned about using my strengths for her own benefit and then "discarded" me from her inner circle once she had gained all the power that she needed. Most of the time they bank on the fact that this black woman is going to stay on and be subdued in the toxic environment because of the difficulty to gain employment. In most black families, it is most likely that this person is the bread winner, not just for the immedate family but also for the broader extended family.

It is extremely important for me to highlight that this is not common behaviour of all the non-whites who are in the "lighter shade of black" group. It is a certain type of individual within the group. This is a very insensitive sect of people who often use their privilege to gain trust and false comradery only to spit you out like the useless fibre of chewed sugar cane that no longer has the sweet flavour. People who have raised and challenged the existence of this phenomenon in general society have been condemned and have been accused of creating division amongst non-whites. Whilst this behaviour is not exhibited by all, it is quite disturbing and destructive.

My point is not to cause divisions but to raise awareness around these individuals who are not necessarily white but also exhibit racist behaviour that is motivated mainly by selfish reasons for their own growth at the expense of those who appear to be the weakest.

When a new black female executive entered one of the organizations that I worked for, she came in with a fresh approach to financial management, asking the right questions that would stimulate the business to improve on efficiencies. It was very interesting to witness how this Pitbull who was "a lighter shade", circled around her, making her feel as though she was her friend, whilst in reality she was threatened by her and was attempting to totally undermine her extensive qualifications and experience. She didn't treat all her other White, Indian and Coloured fellow executives in the same disrespectful way as Black female executives. Because the new executive was asking uncomfortable yet relevant questions, the perpetrator began to tarnish this brilliant black woman's reputation to discredit her. What I found was that given the opportunity, the likes of these individuals become oppressors themselves. Because some of the entities in South Africa operate with an affiliation to another country, an authority country, these Pitbulls abuse the power and ethnic/religious connection that they have to bully and abuse black employees.

Sadly, the discrimination does not end there. The global entities themselves also treat black employees unfairly driven by the Pitbull who often has clout and is highly influential. In the instance where I have been a witness, the global entity would "cancel" black females based on this Pitbull's opinion of them. In one of the global entities, a reign of terror spanning over six months saw more than eight intelligent black women being purged out of the system, some without employment, with the major influencer being the Pitbull.

In my case, I was recruited for a specific mandate within the organization and although I have more in-depth experience within my functional expertise, I later realized that I was assigned a lower grade, which rendered my appointment a demotion vs my previous roles. A 'lighter shade of black' and the cultural advantage worked in my counterpart's favour.

What is also evident is that in order to justify their horrid actions and choices, there was always some mission to dilute the contributions of black people and to steal their ideas whilst instilling so much fear, where they are paralytic to a state that they become poor performers, sabotaging them to the extent of being poor implementers. In these instances, the gate keeper ensures that they stifle your efforts and delay the activities that you are accountable for as a black person. To them there is absolutely no way that a black person can be better. This would mean that you would "steal" their limelight and you would be more successful.

When you dig deeper into the history of this Pitbull, you're more likely to find that they have a history of working with highly successful black men and women where they were almost invisible. Apart from detesting black people, they seem to have an inferiority complex. In this instance, this Pitbull was allegedly let go under the "guise" of being retrenched at an entity, which may have also possibly dented her ego and seemingly left a raw wound that led her to go into a self-preservation and attack mode, in order to protect her position in the organization – striking at the easiest prey. Her strategy seemed to be geared to remove any threats amongst the black people and to disempower those who remained in the business. The sad part is that the global business turned a blind eye and in effect, "co-signed" to her blatant acts of discrimination.

SURVIVAL: SPIRITUAL AND RELIGIOUS GROUNDING

My advice for managing here would be contrary to what someone once advised me which is to 'trust no-one'. I would say 'trust God' because that is what helped me the most in my darkest days (i.e. solid spiritual and religious grounding). Trust your God to sharpen your instincts because in most cases the "red flags" are there from the onset. Look more intently at the way they talk and act toward other black people in lower ranks. Even though they may initially show you support, there are normally some red flags that cannot be ignored. Be cautious especially when you get close to this person because when you're in a position of influence; they may try to dilute your efforts strategically. They have their own stakeholder mapping strategy and are highly committed to engineering their own growth or rise to power at any cost to the black man or woman. They simply don't care!

Make sure that all records are filed accordingly to ensure that your trail is clear. Then build your reputation by being busy - WORK. In my case, I am not good at being an impressionist or building a facade of "knowing it all". For me it has always being about my work "speaking for itself". At one stage a manager said to me: "You are doing an excellent job and I know you like to do your work quietly, but in corporate you need to be 'seen to do' more", meaning that whether you're adding value or not, people, especially those in authority, need to see you being busy – on calls, writing emails, engaging with others and taking charge, in order to create the impression/show that you are working and adding value. I think that to a certain degree this could be true depending on the organizational culture, and whilst I don't completely agree, I believe that there is no harm in trying to improve your Visibility Index, especially in organizations where it counts.

I took the decision to try, in a manner that is true to my values, weighted with integrity, given that I believe it unnecessary to fabricate successes and achievements if one does the work, which is what some impressionists do.

05

ALUTA CONTINUA: *"THE STRUGGLE CONTINUES"*

It was the highlight of my career; I had dreamed of entering that revolving door into the main building of this highly respected global entity many times. I had absolutely no clue of the corporate culture prior to my entry. My exposure was limited to the amazing men and women employees that I had met and engaged with at seminars and conferences as well as at university when I was a student. By the time I strutted into corporate in my modest black mid-heeled shoes, I had already been exposed to the existence of racism in the workplace; however, I was oblivious to the nature and extent of this in corporate South Africa. It didn't take too long for this to become evident especially when a colleague of mine and I registered for our master's degree and were refused funding on the basis that we were not "management material".

The very same white guy who refused to grant us this opportunity was the one who approved for less experienced team members of his kind to be seconded in various roles and for short term assignments outside the country. All this in preparation for acceleration into management roles. This guy wasn't the typical racist Pitbull type with the disadvantage being that it made it very difficult to confront him about his acts of discrimination because of the subtlety. He and my direct line manager at the time, who were both white, were like peas in a pod. Their behaviour was almost identical, always complementary on the surface and in one-on-one conversations where it didn't matter much but being unfair by withholding the benefits and privileges that all are entitled to. Despite the challenges, I was always diligent in my work and a go-getter of note. My role at the time was highly competitive and I worked long hours using innovative means to service my clients to such an extent that I received accolades (awards) from those who were regarded amongst the most difficult to manage.

What was interesting was that the ones that I connected with the most and that loved me the most were of Afrikaner descent. What they had to say about my work and overall service was heart-wrenching. In direct contrast to this was an Afrikaner lady, the second pea in the pod, whose behaviour can be described in isiZulu as: "Uyaluma ephephetha" which means that she depicted subtle racist behaviour and actions that were meant to stunt my career whilst at the same time she would behave respectfully toward me at face value and shower me with compliments. She seemed very cordial and would often ask me if I was okay. At some point it felt as though she was nurturing toward me, and I fell for it because she seemed to make me feel as though I was the best in the team, to the point of assigning me "deputized" tasks.

Deep down in our hearts a lot of us seek validation, especially if in other areas of our lives this is not forthcoming, we tend to seek that validation elsewhere, especially in the workplace where many workers spend most of their time. Sometimes those spaces are not the best of spaces and leave room for the abuse of power. This very lady (mentioned earlier) could not create good presentations or reports and could not articulate herself professionally on email. She could manoeuvre her way around business conversations based on her experience; however, she relied on me for the administrative and creative side of her role.

She would pull me from the field strategically around month end when it was time to submit reports which I would complete to the best of my abilities at the office since we didn't have laptops back then. At some stage she would just give me her latest login details and I would send the reports to Head Office directly in her name. It became a standing joke in the office that she would always deliberately plan her trips out of the office at such a critical period of the month. I would somehow be blinded by her immense display of gratitude. She would thank me profusely and comment about how brilliant I was and how valuable of an asset I was for the organization.

She used to get such complements on how well her work was presented and won an award at some point, which I was ecstatic about. Sadly, when it really mattered the most her true loyalty and affinity were revealed. When it came to giving accolades and opportunities, only my white colleagues were considered and blatantly given all the awards. What didn't make sense was that externally I was getting accolades, with customers bestowing me with "Supplier of the Year" and commendations, the only one to receive this ever, in the Division and function. This happened quite often where black employees were overlooked to such an extent that the rules seemed to change to suit the mission to "cheat" us out of recognition. Given that at the local office all my colleagues knew what my input was and I was still being overlooked – this was astonishing and hurtful at the same time. This was my first encounter with a Snake in corporate. Whilst not as venomous as some of those that I was to meet later in my journey, this had a major impact on me in terms of trust. As if the awards were not enough, she then promoted my less experienced, more junior colleague, whom I had assisted in training and at some point, I eventually had to report to her.

For me that was the last straw and I reported this, raising my concerns with the head of department and HR. I guess looking back now I realise that I probably should have followed a more formal process because whilst they all acknowledged that this was not right, nothing was done about it. The learning is to follow the formal process because if it doesn't affect them directly people don't prioritize your cause. The other learning was that when people get away with these discriminatory acts, they will most likely do it again, to you and others.

You cannot ignore excellence for too long and I worked twice as hard in the subsequent years to the extent that I received global awards and was eventually promoted. This didn't mean that I was safe though because at the height of my tenure I was earmarked for a global assignment (I was later informed by a reliable source) which was given to another white lady who had initially reported to me. This catapulted her career to amazing heights whilst I was shamelessly set aside. I think that what hurt me the most back then was the knowledge that a life changing opportunity that would have changed my family's life was given to someone else because of the colour of my skin. How evil does one have to be to shamelessly take a golden opportunity from another! Discrimination of any kind is evil.

What I am grateful for is the presence of good people in the unlikeliest of places, who gave me hope and kept me sane. Whilst my other black colleagues and I experienced racism there were some guardian angels who were there in the periphery, who kept me going. There was this older white lady in an adjacent support function that was paramount in the fate of my projects, with whom I developed a bond based on mutual respect for each other's work ethic.

She would always comment about how she appreciated my approach and respect for her role. She appreciated me for who I am as a professional with no mind to the colour of my skin. She and her team would sometimes do me favours to make sure that I don't fail. I could tell that they always felt bad for me when I was unfairly treated. They voiced this when I eventually left the organization and to date some of them communicate with me from time to time. She forms part of a tribe of women who became an unlikely support structure in my career, women who continue to care.

HOW I MANAGED

At the most challenging of times, I performed at my peak with the **assistance of another set of women** who again looked more at what I had to offer versus the colour of my skin. This was to an extent that I received supplier awards because of these trailblazers who drove the industry and never compromised on the standards of quality and outputs, even in the selection and recognition of service in excellence. I really needed to know what I was talking about with these ladies because they were very learned as academics, with a wealth of experience.

For me this forms part of the advice to manage internal racism, **excelling in what you do** in such a way that it cannot be ignored, supported by key external stakeholders. In my case, this most certainly made a difference in that I left an undeniable trail in terms of proof of performance that leaves the racist Pitbull with no choice but to give credit where it's due. Racist internal stakeholders could not deny me the independent external accolades supported by the internal data that measured my performance. This was one of my major strategies which kept me going and built my integrity. I built my personal brand outside of the organization to such an extent that it filtered back inwards.

06

HIGH ON
POWER

"It came to pass" that I landed at this global organization all "bright eyed and bushy tailed", ecstatic at being selected from several candidates. I went through all the rigorous assessments that this organization needed to screen and to eventually source whom they deemed to be the best and final candidate suitable for the role. They chose "Yours Truly", which was me. I knew that I would be dealing with a tough "cookie", my new boss, from the interviews and selection process, which reminds me of the process of entering new territory as you are scrutinised and even singled out for more intense scrutiny before entry.

When I met the female Pitbull for the second time as a new employee, within a short space of time I could tell that she was one of the very privileged, clearly still very immature for the position in leadership, a product of white privilege who had been moved up the ranks too quickly, based on the colour of her skin. During the recruitment process, we managed to have a cheerful discussion, though seemingly forced, however, on joining the team officially the true character showed up in full. On that first day it seemed as though her Alta Ego had walked into the room, from the facial expression to the tone of voice, leaving no doubt as to who was in charge. This racist Pitbull went into character rather quickly as if to mark her territory.

They say that dogs urinate over certain spots of a property to mark their territory and show who is in charge and her behaviour was reminiscent of this. I was left with my jaw ajar at what I found in her department, in an organization that I believed was progressive in terms of diversity. Those who were part of the team back then gave me some insights into her background after a few weeks of my tenure. It seemed as though she was born into a conservative racist family which made matters worse, given that she already had issues stemming from life experiences that resulted in her low self-esteem. The minute I walked into the departmental office I knew that I had fallen into a segregated "war zone" just by looking at the seating arrangement. "Was it a coincidence or was it based on seniority?"... I asked myself. I was surprised to find that this "apartheid style" practice was orchestrated by the Pitbull herself. The Teacher's Pet (who was also white) was given the prime spot at the corner of the open-plan office and the only other white person also occupied the second corner with both spaces being larger than the rest and the only ones that had a window view. They were given prime spots without any logical explanation other than the fact that they were the only two white team members. I couldn't believe that such blatant discrimination existed to this extent in that era, and no one seemed to be decent and bold enough to deal with it directly.

Being a "newbie", I didn't want to interfere immediately and didn't mention my observations to anyone at first, lest I be labeled a troublemaker. I eventually questioned this at some point when there were several other elements that made it apparent that racism did exist, and it had become unbearable for many of us. The pattern was that the highest-ranking black team member would be the worst affected as if to send a strong message to the rest to "tow the line". I discovered that I wasn't the first victim, that my brilliant predecessor who later became a very good friend of mine was also a victim of the Pitbull. This was clearly a missed opportunity for the business given that the very same black professional woman eventually occupied some of the most senior roles in our country, in corporate and government, making an impact on our communities and the SA economy.

The Pitbull had treated her so badly that when she left to relocate with her family within a year, it was a welcome relief. At some point she had made remarks around her annunciation of the English language saying that she spoke English "like the Chinese", and smirking about it at that! We sometimes joke about this as friends when we discuss our struggles in corporate, marvelling at how a naturally beautiful African accent could be equated to a Chinese accent in a derogatory manner. The words were meant to demean, demotivate, and destroy her self-esteem along with the other acts of racism; however, from what I witnessed first-hand, it made her stronger and she has given many in the same situation some hope. Pitbulls are often actually quite delusional in that they often believe that they own your future outside the organization in which they may manage you and that they can destroy your career. What they may well do is to leave scars; however, they most certainly are not in control of your future victories.

My story with this very same racist Pitbull who had ill-treated my friend unfolded, as I unknowingly became her next target. I marvelled at the way she unapologetically singled me out and would randomly ask me "trick" questions that would enable her to ridicule me in front of my peers. She was a vile, evil human being who had no mercy even when I was clearly downtrodden. I had joined the organization having graduated with an MBA, a contrast to hers which had been limited to a basic qualification. I personally admire and do not judge people based on their certificates, whether few or many and was sad to find yet another white individual displaying signs of an inferiority complex, because of my hard-earned qualifications. It reminded me of what a previous boss once said: "You black people study too much! Your certificates won't do anything for you!" One could argue that they're entitled to their opinions; however, this becomes a problem when it is seemingly a trigger for resentment. Whose fault was it that she didn't invest her time and money on furthering her education vs choosing to travel across the world? I am a keen traveller myself and I believe that there is much to be gained from immersing oneself in other cultures. Why wasn't this satisfactory as a source for education and an enriching life experience? Why source someone of a high calibre only to try and tame them to your required specification? No black person reporting to this lady had ever been promoted during her tenure in the organization, whereas all our white colleagues were promoted under the guise of evolving portfolios.

This was very demotivating for the few remaining black individuals in the team; however, we still managed to carry each other, encouraging each other to strive for excellence despite the challenges. Our comradery pulled us through the worst of times, and I remember so many times where I would come out of the racist Pitbull's office feeling like a complete idiot and I would come face to face with the black receptionist sitting outside her office who always made the blows feel so much less damaging. She gave me hope by telling me the stories of other victims like me, other "survivors". A young black lady who had been written off as a failure under the Pitbull's reign went on to complete her MBA and became a leading force in strategic marketing in the banking sector.

The other example is one who left corporate and became a successful entrepreneur in the energy sector whilst creating her own successful clothing brand.

The question is: "What was the modus operandi of this Pitbull and how did one overcome this era, the challenges that were presented in this destination?" Picture yourself in a packed boardroom full of your colleagues and external agency partners and you're presenting or giving feedback to a creative piece. As an individual I have always had pride in the fact that I strive for excellence and take pride in my work. Imagine how gutted I would feel after a session in a room full of learned people where I was intellectually humiliated by the Pitbull. This was not my first rodeo with a Pitbull, however, this was even worse. This woman would find every and any opportunity to embarrass me especially to key stakeholders and given the fact that I didn't have enough history, she would succeed. She openly treated white people differently and I later discovered that she would go out with them privately after hours and had exclusive agreements regarding career progression that didn't exist for black employees. I discovered this accidently when I went out with a white colleague to a pub. She drank a little too much alcohol and eventually "spilt the beans". It turns out that she and the Pitbull had a special long-standing agreement around her remuneration and succession plan which was outside the norm. She had lied for the Pitbull in a disciplinary case where the Pitbull would have definitely been fired.

I was shocked and realised then that there was definitely no hope of succession here. I also discovered that the other white colleague was the Pitbull's family friend and that their families sometimes had braais over the weekend. The odds were against us. Apart from being detested for being black there were possibly so many other deep unknown secrets and factors that we were not aware of that made us enemies.

HOW I MANAGED

It is important to leave this destination with the key learnings that will help others and equip them for their next destination.

Striving for Excellence - in my struggles during my tenure I ensured that I do not falter in terms of my delivery, across the board. Whilst I was suffering from the public humiliation meted out to me, I ensured that I had a good track record in terms of project management and was very blessed to work with and be supported by an excellent team. Each and every one of the agencies that I worked with gave raving reviews for my 360-degree feedback to the extent that one of the Managing Directors (MD), who is now a dollar billionaire in his own right, is my character reference to this day and is a good friend. Further to this is the fact that because of the work done with external players I won a prestigious global award. Whilst I was not completely free from the clutches of racism, with these accolades I was somewhat protected from being unfairly classified as a poor performer.

Understanding my rights - I have outlined the disappointment that has come with dealing with HR practitioners who were incapable of dealing with racism head on. In this scenario the HR leader was unfortunately a Chicken; however, the situation changed when a feisty black woman was brought into his department. What I loved about her was that she was candid and treated everyone equally. She became my "go-to" person in terms of policy and understanding my rights. In essence, finding an ally in the HR department helps, even if it's just to verify what your rights are. In my case, the knowledge gave me the courage to open up and stand up for myself.

Speaking Out - inherently I am someone who speaks

out against social ills, with discrimination of any kind being high up on the agenda. Speaking out not only helps in terms of raising an alarm to atrocities taking place, it also helps the individual mentally somewhat, as it did with me. There might not be much that is done at that very moment whilst you are in the employ of the organization; however, I always encourage people to speak out, especially because of the changes that eventually take place because of your contribution, as was previously documented.

Another way is calling out overt racism when you witness it. I recall a newly appointed white lady came to the department and allocated tasks to groups according to race groups, blatantly assigning the menial undesirable tasks to the group of black team members. I remember walking into the office straight to the lady's desk, informing her of my observations and that this was not how things are to be done in this day and age. She reported me to the Pitbull who could not deal with me directly because I had regained my power by then, through courage and excellence. By then I had also gained respect and clout in the global teams, which formed an additional layer of protection. She was advised to set up a meeting with me and to apologise, which she did and as only I could do, I promptly asked her to apologise to my black colleagues as well, which she did. News spreads fast in corporate especially small offices and so, when I came to the office the next day, I discovered that word of our encounter had spread and no one else ever attempted such henceforth.

Stakeholder Mapping - I must admit that I'm not good with this. This refers to consciously ensuring that I have relations with the key stakeholders in the organization. My mapping has always been around those whom I work with directly and who I report to. In this instance I was very blessed in that I was in a small office where the MD was fair and accessible (an Eagle in many ways). He treated everyone equally, from the cleaner to the directors of the company. As an example, when we worked late in the evenings, he would buy us all who were present dinner, irrespective of your position – a simple yet meaningful gesture.

I do believe that because of the relationship that I had with him in my own right I was somewhat protected in that he would be able to vouch for me where my name would be mentioned in a negative manner. Therefore, my advice is to go as far as you can in terms of aligning with key stakeholders. I might not be an expert on this myself; however, I do believe that there is merit in trying. For me it's a key area that I am willing to navigate further and learn.

07

BLACK BRAINS
MATTER

Iwent to the next destination with such excitement and eagerness to make a huge difference in my motherland, especially given that this organization was home-grown and renowned for understanding what the masses need and how to fill the gaps. They were a local giant with brands and products that were leaders across their segments, very much loved by Africans.

Whilst working for a multinational I saw an innovation by this giant, a traditional product that they had commercialized to save on costs and time for people. I was bowled over and immediately called my recruitment agent and asked her to find me a position there, which she did. I remember telling her that all I needed was for her to get me to interview stage and the job would be mine!

This is where I met two of the most amazing characters in my career, a boss lady who was the epitome of excellence, integrity and grit (an Eagle) as well as an HR manager who was ahead of the game amongst his peers in terms of employee relations, with a good balance in terms of business deliverables. I knew from the onset that he could be trusted given his frank and honest responses to my questions during the interview, he didn't try to make the organization look like the perfect setting that didn't exist; which often leads to disappointment.

Landing at this organization felt more like a home-coming. I walked into those wide sliding doors with a pep on my step and the widest of smiles, to the warmest welcome. The MD came down personally to welcome me from the reception area together with the young lady that was going to report to me. I could tell that this was not a common occurrence just based on the reaction from the receptionists. What humility from a leader though? I knew that I had made the right decision. This was home.

Over the years this brilliant yet humble individual would become a source of inspiration. My experience was different here, being led by two strong black women who shielded the team where necessary and were always ready to recognize excellence. I found that these two incredible women were also able to channel talent in the relevant spaces to add value to the business. For example, they knew that I was motivated and inspired by new projects and for that reason they would include me in innovation projects for the whole division. The MD was so dedicated to nurturing talent that when the business would not fund my trip to an innovation expo in Europe, she offered to use her personal resources to fund the same. Whilst there were pockets of racism in the organization, I had not been impacted directly until there was a change in leadership. My then direct boss moved on and a racist female Pitbull took over. This is when access to the MD also became an issue and was limited. The change was sudden and the consequences unexpected.

In a previous chapter I referred to the story of my botched wedding experience, which transpired because of the antics of a racist Pitbull at this organization. It took place at the height of my tenure at what I thought would be a dream destination.

A very prominent member of the family was getting married in one of the most beautiful destinations, Franschhoek, where the bill to get married goes to millions of rands. Our relative, a prominent government official was marrying a renowned female business executive and as such the guest list included government officials (including the SA president) as well as top businesspeople that included the wealthiest man in Africa, at the time. With that type of networking opportunity, the expectation would be that I would be at my best both mentally and in how I presented myself. Not on the Pitbull's watch!

Somehow, I knew from the onset that we were not going to get along given her track record with black people. She was notorious for her racist attitude and behaviours, and I had called her out once on this in a group setting, which I don't think she had forgotten, the source of my disastrous soapie.

There were many incidences that one could narrate; however, this wedding remains the most prominent in my mind because of the various levels of emotions that were triggered.

It's a few days before the wedding and the Pitbull calls me to her office and asks me to complete a document that normally takes weeks to prepare. For me that wasn't a problem at all, the problem was that she expected me to complete this document in record time knowing full well that I was going to this wedding. By then it was not surprising that she would disregard my plans; however, I was a little taken aback that she would trust me to complete such a key document given that she had put me through so much humiliation during her tenure both privately and publicly and was already trying to taint my image with HR executives. She was systematically trying to position me as an angry black woman who was refusing to respect her and to be managed by a white woman. The day I realised the extent of her actions was when I was called in by another executive from a different function who appreciated my work and he asked me what the issue was because whatever our issue was, it was becoming personal and very uncomfortable to watch during team meetings. His role in my story of survival within the organisation was immense.

The big wedding weekend comes and I'm working full steam on the document that the Pitbull wants to be completed ASAP. I found this to be ironic given her attempts to make me look incompetent, and yet she trusted with such an important project, demanding near instant delivery. This was confusing; however, the agenda was a very selfish one, as will be revealed. Picture me typing away at the OR Tambo International Airport, on the flight to Cape Town, enroute to Franschhoek and only lifting my head to get the necessary security clearance for the wedding. I can't even remember checking into one of the most beautiful places in SA and only really realising what I had missed after the fact. What I remember is how worried I was about completing the document before morning and sending it to the Pitbull. She wanted to have it by midnight that Friday and I ended up sending it through by 5am the following morning.

Although I don't recall getting a "Thank You", I believe that it was near perfect because nothing was changed after she read through it over the weekend. She only added a title page and signed her name at the end.

In an instant my sacrifice, a tainted experience became null and void, all for nothing and the work of my hands became the intellectual property of a racist Pitbull. Mind you, I wasn't looking my best at the wedding of the century because I didn't even have time to do my nails, my hair and my make up. Over and above this, what was an opportunity to network with highflyers was ruined because I was totally exhausted and had bags under my eyes.

As previously mentioned, I could only hope that I looked presentable and that my mother's genes, that natural beauty, would save the day. Because I didn't feel at my best, I have a limited number of photos of the day and with the few that I have, I do still get reminded of the Pitbull and her impact on me. This also happens every time I drive past Franschhoek and as part of my healing process, I decided to spend a vacation in the very same place, somewhat taking back what I was robbed of.

The story of the wedding didn't just end there, the Pitbull not only takes credit for the words that were created by my brain, but she "crucifies" me and forbids me from using my own words! As content creators one would relate to the fact that once you've completed a master document it is common practice to modify and use extracts from there for other documents and presentations, which I did based on projects. Because she had claimed the work as her own, I believe that the Pitbull was embarrassed that others would recognize that the work that she would later present as her own was not hers and that I had completed the document, hence her dismay when she recognized the content.

I remember getting a call from the Pitbull immediately after sending out an email with a project charter that I had prepared including extracts from the main document. I had never heard her sounding so livid about anything before and although I did explain that this was a project charter for the same category where the issues had to be outlined, she still sent me a nasty email of reprimand, though struggling to articulate the violation. Needless to say, it still didn't stop her from sending my document as her own to the board of directors without acknowledging my input. The rewarding element from all of this was that given the positive response from the board, I was quite certain that my skills were not questionable, which boosted my confidence.

The attacks continued; the racist Pitbull had enough gall to try to demean me as a human being through her constant acts of sabotage which became worse after the incident. The public humiliation and attempts to impact my career negatively were endless. Going to work became a daily struggle for me. Although the experience was a bittersweet one given the acknowledgement of my work. The wrath of terror intensified so much after that episode that I even reported this to my MD and the head of HR at the time, only to be disappointed at the response. I was on my own, with the only reason I survived being that I developed my own survival strategy. At least what I knew for sure was that my integrity and the work of these hands of mine were solid.

The wrath of a Pitbull scorned is nothing short of lethal, it is vile and potentially paralysing. I learnt this the hard way. After landing perfectly in that fertile home-grown strip and experiencing the most heart-warming of work lives I had ever had in my career, it felt as though a foreign settler had invaded the mother land, creating an environment where they were forcefully demanding submission and meting out punishment for any glimpse of brilliance and courage that emerged. Any such "shine" or special moment would be at risk of being stolen without any conscience. In addition to all of this, the perpetrator borrowed so much from her racist forefathers that took control of our country for decades and went as far as using two of my fellow black sisters as pawns to source information about me in order to find fault with my work. It reiterated how real the struggle in corporate still is, with racism still being rife and some of our black brothers and sisters being used as pawns, becoming part of the plot in the demise of other black people. I have often wondered how the minds of these people work. How do you even begin to orchestrate the fall of your brother or sister let alone watching them die inside as they become oppressed, and the screws are tightened by the racist Pitbulls of this world. The first one was a baby Snake who totally blindsided me after I had given her a lease in life. Destitute and coming from a very abusive marriage, a colleague and I made her our "special project" ensuring that she becomes mentally stable and recovers in all aspects of her life including gaining financial freedom. She had been trying to get back into corporate unsuccessfully for many years and this was her big break after a disaster, not because the family business was not thriving, but because of the extreme abuse that she experienced from her controlling partner.

I was approached by the colleague regarding her situation, and I decided to help especially with her technical skills being inadequate for the role at the time. I had to put in extra effort to get the work done and to help improve her technical skills at the same time. What I didn't bank on was that when the Pitbull was in full steam attack mode this very same woman would be roped in to help in orchestrating my demise. Although I was very hurt by her actions, I actually still treated her normally until the very end and even prayed for her after she surprisingly bawled her eyes out at my departure. The second was a full-grown Snake, a colleague who was very close to the Pitbull because of their history. She would add fuel to the fire in terms of making my relationship with the Pitbull even worse. This lady was notorious in the industry for being "shady" and I had consciously avoided working anywhere near her. This time I had no choice because she joined the team, and I would be subjected to the results of her many schemes to get ahead by stepping on the shoulders of others. The situation was just messy, a story of lies and sabotage. I remember how I learnt that she systematically drew the small Snake in to jointly crafting a web of lies that would cause me great discomfort. I praise God for the brain and work ethic which was eventually quite instrumental in ensuring that I deliver above and beyond the call of duty.

I must admit that there were days when I felt like giving up, however, my strong faith in God gave me the strength to carry on. I just wouldn't allow racists to bully me and overwhelm me with their bullying into a state of paralysis. After a while, the victimization can become exasperating, which makes it important to have a strong spiritual grounding and good support. The mind can either be an architect to your destruction or can be the solid rock that you need to keep your sanity, and to be focused.

Because I inherently believe in the good of people, I was quite shocked at the extent that Pitbulls would go to, to destroy you once I discovered the scheme that was going on behind my back. With them there is absolutely no room for one to let their guard down, there is no mercy. I often asked myself a few questions alone at night and wondered what victory would look like in their eyes because they didn't seem to let go even during the worst of times, when you were down and out.

Here is another demonstration of their antics. Budgets are a sensitive subject in any business, and it so happened that the trio managed to get me embroiled where I was never supposed to be. The Snake was careless in managing her own budget and tried to blame others including myself. This threatened the wellbeing of the innocent (including me) and our survival in the organization; however, I was the only one who openly retaliated to the extent that my colleagues called it a "career limiting move". To add to this the small Snake completely changed the story around budget commitments made previously, placing me in a compromised position. The situation was dire in that I could have been given a final written warning for a fabricated case. After protesting, justice prevailed and I am glad to report that my innocent colleagues and I were cleared, and the racist Pitbull never succeeded in tainting my hard-earned sterling reputation at that organization. My reputation remained solid such that my relationship with the Group Executives remained solid even after I had left the organization.

Yes, I can acknowledge that there were times where I was extremely hurt and felt so humiliated that I wished that I didn't need to go back to those offices. By God's grace I was able to manage all those challenging situations that I encountered, enough to leave a lasting impression.

HOW I MANAGED

A few additions to the tactics outlined earlier in terms of what assisted me in coping:

Passion for the craft - it is often said that having passion for your work energizes you and keeps you focused in the most challenging of times. This helped me immensely during the toughest of times. It is only when that spark for the brand or organization has dimmed that I started considering leaving the organization. This was a rarity that was only made possible by acts of extreme racism that are soul breaking.

Leveraging key relationships - although I was not really good at lobbying, in this organization I managed to become close to 2 key stakeholders, which included the Group Functional Head (GFH) and the Customer Executive (CE). The GFH became very instrumental in managing my reputation at group level, especially given that I was privileged to be involved in key group projects. The second key stakeholder was the CE who was actually closely involved in my appointment. This meant that I would be a few steps ahead in terms of customer insights and it did make a difference. Whenever he could, the CE would also attempt to come to the rescue by stepping in on my behalf during meetings when I was being humiliated. I'll never forget that guy – may his beautiful soul rest in peace.

As part of the strategy to elevate my stature to build personal and team equity I encouraged the team to seek external recognition which included recognition of the brands that I was responsible for as well as the calibre of partnerships and engagement with external stakeholders. These achievements were to be published internally in the business or mentioned in business reports, business planning meetings and other key forums. I believe that this is part of the internal PR that is helpful in protecting and building your personal brand within the organization.

08

EMPOWERED: LEGACY
IN PARADISE

Lights, camera, action! This was the scene at the glamorous Beverley Hills Hotel nestled in upmarket Umhlanga, along the KZN coast. It was one of those prestigious events that advertising agencies and magazines put together to showcase the opportunities that are available for brands for the short and long term.

One of the top magazines in the country organized this huge occasion to present their latest offering, introduce their new editor and to unveil their latest cover. The decor, the menu, guest speakers and overall ambience of the venue clearly showed that no funds were spared to host this event. As we sat at our VIP tables all dressed to the nines with our names marked and placed in front of each of us, one of the ladies seated across unexpectedly blurted: "Oh it's you!" This was just before the formalities commenced whist people were socialising. Because I didn't recognize her, I looked to my left and right to see who she was talking to. It was quite evident that she was talking to me. I believe that she could see my puzzled look because she stood up and made her way around the table towards me. She didn't make it on time, though, and promptly turned back to her seat; however, before she sat down, she made a gesture to inform me that she would talk to me later. Now I was really intrigued and curious as to how she knew me and wondered when the first break would be so that she could unravel the mystery.

By the time it was the first comfort break I was more than eager to have a conversation with her. This young lady blurted, "So you are the legendary one!" Legendary, that's a big word; what did she mean? She was holding my hand as she was speaking to me as if she knew me, and she was telling me of how she had heard so many stories about me at the company where she worked. "There's never a day that we don't hear a story about you or just talk about you!" Those were the words that I found hard to believe because to me it just did not seem possible for a nobody like me to be on the lips of so many and so often. I remember asking: "What do you talk about? Is it good or bad?" She went on to explain how the actions that I had taken during my tenure at her company had resulted in fundamental changes in the policies and the way that black people were being treated. For example, for the first time, black women were even considered for global assignments. "Because you spoke out against racism, conditions improved considerably, and we are now enjoying the fruits of your labour, your courage. People tell me that our current boss is totally different to the nasty person that she was before you came. She treated black people very, very harshly back then. So, I believe we have you to thank! " This was a complete surprise for me, a pleasant one at that because I had never known prior to this encounter whether the actions that I had taken back then had made an impact.

Had my pain and suffering been worth it? This seemed to be the case.

I came from another province to join this well-renowned global company after going through a rigorous selection process that saw me travelling to and from their head offices for several months. I was told that it had been difficult to find the right person and that everyone was thrilled to have me there, which turned out to be untrue.

Upon arrival on my first day at the office I was greeted by two white ladies who were my new colleagues, to be revealed at a later stage as the Snake and Teacher's Pet in this part of my journey. They began circling me from day 1! I wasn't aware of this back then and I was merely relieved that on my first day, I was welcomed with an intimate coffee at the nearest restaurant; and a reassurance of support during my on-boarding and beyond. I was thrilled that I was not going to be burdened with the anxiety of newness in a role that was very senior, having relocated to a new city as well. My colleagues went all out to show care and I felt that I was set to deliver on the mandate that lay ahead, which was to change the face of the said brands' efforts in advertising to showcase the true essence of the masses of South Africa. Little did I know that the storm began brewing the minute I walked into the front door. The vultures, Snakes, Pitbulls and every other racist predator was waiting to tear me apart at the most opportune moment. For the Teacher's Pet and the Snake, the strategy was simple, be nice to her, extract as much information as you can from her and then strike hard enough to neutralize her and frustrate her out of the system. Little did they know that this girl born and bred in Thula Road, Machibisa had the grit to fight back long enough to raise the alarm of racism that was being swept under that huge carpet at the entrance hall of the building. The humiliating scenes that were being played out against black people behind those walls were quite hurtful. Being amongst the few blacks at senior management level wasn't easy especially during discussions about black subordinates whom I felt were being targeted unfairly.

There was a lone white lady who was fair during those discussions, and I would later hear that she had voiced out her disgust at some point, at how I and others were treated because of our race. She would consistently be my ally whether I was in the room or not and we later ended up working on projects beyond this company after we had both left.

My tenure started off on a good note and I was gaining respect on a local and global level to the extent that I represented the African continent at a game changing conference within a short space of time. The situation started going South when the Snake and the Teacher's Pet started behaving strangely toward me and did all they possibly could to unleash the wrath of the racist Pitbull (my then boss) against me. Hated once again for having the combination of being an intelligent black woman brought in to add value to a system that was otherwise lacking in the current realities. At some point I heard that the trio was annoyed because I seemed to "hold back" in their presence and would share my knowledge only in meaningful forums where I would stand out and shine. I seemingly didn't understand that I needed to transfer knowledge to this trio, and they would then be the stars to unearth the insights that they had miserably failed to unearth previously.

To be honest this was not a deliberate ploy to outplay them, they just weren't listening carefully and bordering on being dismissive at times. They didn't seem to realise that the expertise that I brought with me could not be transmitted via osmosis. This was experience accumulated over years and years of work on the ground, sometimes under harsh circumstances, complemented by formal education. Nevertheless, the trio would meet without informing me to prepare for key meetings which I would be informed of at the last minute, and

I would be told to "just bring your brain" every time I asked what I needed to prepare. These were the most uncomfortable meetings that I attended especially when I realised that I had been duped, and that the Snake and Teacher's Pet had prepared beautiful presentations to share. On the first few occasions I managed to "wing it" at these meetings; however, it came to a point where the Pitbull called me on a Wednesday to tell me that I was presenting to the executive team in two days, on that Friday. This was in the middle of a major shoot for a television commercial that was out of town. The brief from the Pitbull was very sketchy, and as such I put together a business case using the standard template, with key information that the business commonly used for decision making. The Pitbull was privy to all this; however, she didn't support me at all at the leadership meeting; the executive team crucified me.

I allegedly had not followed the new procedure for presenting to the leaders (which I was unaware of) and had also focused on detail that was no longer important for this case, based on previous discussions with the Pitbull. What was shocking was that she agreed with them and made me look like a fool although she had failed to give me a proper brief as a new incumbent.

Apparently, she felt very threatened and intimidated starting from the selection process and had been overruled by the rest of the panel to appoint me. She could not give the panel a good enough reason not to appoint me over a white candidate that had previously been in their employ and had begrudgingly agreed to my appointment. I told her after my appointment how intimidating she had been at the interview with executives, when she crossed her arms to show her annoyance toward the CEO who was oozing "love" and showing great interest in my career. A one-hour appointment extended to a further two-hour discussion with the then CEO. This didn't sit well with my new boss.

It's fair to say that I had landed in foreign territory that was riddled with landmines. Despite the many explosions that were meant to break my spirit I still managed to make a difference. I alerted HR management and the MD regarding the racist atrocities of the Pitbull on numerous occasions and right within sight of HR at times, with no fear. Nothing was done about her racist behaviour. She went on to oust most of the black staff and would blatantly praise and reward only the white staff. What was also clear was that it was only white staff who could resign and be privileged with positions as consultants after their tenure was over.

It all came to a head one day when there was a confrontation in the Pitbull's office, where I went ahead, and I told her that she was a racist. She made it worse when she told me about the number of black friends that she has and how close she was to her black helper. It was too much for me and I remember leaving the room immediately. She missed the point, which was to stop discrimination in the team. I knew then that I had to take drastic measures! I remember saying to her: "Ooooooh, that is exactly what racists say". Our relationship deteriorated further from there and the acts of sabotage from the racist trio escalated. I reported this to the MD again and because I was not taken seriously, I wrote a heart-felt letter to the executive team regarding racism in the organization and the long-term impact that it had on black employees and their families. I had also resigned, and the Pitbull literally ran to the MD and HR offices to ensure that they would refrain from giving me any counteroffers. It wasn't a hard task as I later discovered, the Pitbull and her boss, the CEO were close family friends to the extent that they owned holiday property together and went on long vacations together. She wanted to ensure that the thorn, the "clever black" would disappear and she would have her way without being challenged. It didn't matter to her that I had the courage to expose racism against the backdrop of glass walls and doors, presenting an opportunity for change, the acceptance of embracing diversity and making a change for the better.

I dealt with it the best way I know how, by using the voice and courageous spirit that God had bestowed over me. I wrote a heartfelt letter to the executive team highlighting the blatant acts of racism in the organization (included in Chapter 9).

HOW I MANAGED

Being courageous - I have always known since I joined corporate that the job of the black man and woman in fighting discrimination is not over! Keeping silent about this would become the fuel to the destruction of my soul, apart from the fact that there's a missed opportunity to pave the way for future generations. I say, have the courage to speak out or write your thoughts out to those around you that are influential, in their exact form as I have done. Call it what it is, racism, the destructive remnants that remain in the post - apartheid era.

Building an inner circle - build a strong network of supporters by identifying with key stakeholders early on, especially globally so that the situation can be dealt with early. Global offices are often sensitive to the issues that could potentially impact their reputation, that do not reflect their values. I discovered this very late when I was already "boarding" my next flight to the next destination, my next career move. Ensuring that you extend your support base early empowers you and helps to protect your corporate well-being and makes the journey from survival to thriving easier.

Living a Healthy Lifestyle - I remember huffing and puffing in the streets of a foreign land whilst playing the "Amazing Race" and

I was miserable about my work environment, about my body and that's when I decided to take charge. I was at a low point, and this was going to be a Body, Mind and Spirit intervention. This was my turning point! Although I had been attending church, my relationship with God had been on autopilot mode for a while. I elevated this relationship in many ways, praying and fasting, serving in the church, and seeking counsel from my leaders.

My relationship with my body and food became healthier. I lived the ELLAGENCE Mantra which is "Love the foods that love you back!" I joined a studio gym and rekindled my love for healthier foods. I lost the excess weight and embraced my body anew. This renewed self-care and self-love, following my passion by giving of my time and resources helped to boost my confidence and to remove me from the negative space that the racism in corporate was taking me. I began a holistic health journey which I have shared with the world, empowering others and which has elevated me beyond my expectations.

09

THRIVING BEYOND
SURVIVAL

Thriving beyond survival requires purpose and a great deal of courage. As I sat in the middle of the various points of my destination, between destinations, manoeuvring my way from organizations that didn't and still don't have empathy for black people; I didn't lose the fire to fight back even if it was the smallest gesture that would trigger change. I can safely say that in every organization where I witnessed discrimination of any kind, I reported it in one way or another whether it be directly to the authorities or documented in the form of a letter. Although not 100% exact for legal reasons, this is an example of what I once wrote to executives of a global entity (named Terminus for the purpose of this book).

THE TITLE

"Perfect Landing Wrong Airport -
*My Journey, My Passage Through *Terminus"*

THE BODY

"As human beings we are equipped with senses that enable us to discern the most defining moments and experiences in life and I can safely say that my tenure at Terminus has been one such experience in many ways. I came to Terminus with aspirations of creating a long-term partnership that would enable the company to move to the next level in terms of winning the hearts of SA and securing a prosperous future for Terminus in SA. The most important aspect for me was that I myself had "fallen in love" with the organization and its people, based on my exchanges with some of the people that were at the forefront of securing my engagement. I realized very quickly that I was part of something really special under the leadership of a strong and (very importantly) humane leader with a great team to help steer this "ship".

I met all the members of the Executive team outside of marketing individually as well and was ecstatic and confident that I would be working and learning; drawing on their experiences and balancing this with the experience and knowledge that I was bringing to the organization. This feeling was further fuelled in the months to come whilst in Terminus HQ (global office) attending the Annual Expo where I came back feeling really proud of being associated with the organization. Although the mandate and task ahead seemed like quite a mammoth task, I felt safe. I had full confidence and trust that I would receive enough guidance and support to steer me through this HUGE transition.

There were many elements to be managed in terms of changes that came with this engagement - that all parties were aware of, including amongst other:

1. The large portfolio to manage (a multitude of brands)
2. The mandate to help crack the Black market in general (an exciting prospect
3. A team in transition requiring guidance and with varying challenges (including inadequate manpower) and;
4. Challenged leader(ship)

This was the scenario from the onset of my tenure and although this was a tremendously "big ask" under the circumstances, my faith and trust in the organization was unwavering.

*What transpired thereafter in the subsequent months was a mixed bag - quite tumultuous to say the least. There are many special moments and achievements that I can list, particularly the involvement with global initiatives that I believe are in line with the mandate to have a breakthrough in Black ***n and the great performance of my portfolio under trying circumstances including vicious competition.*

With that being said and given the circumstances under which I was employed (which I have listed above) my tenure became short of a traumatic experience. I remember quite clearly articulating to my immediate manager quite early and in May (+ subsequent to this) that I felt as though I was "catching the ball that was closest to the ground" meaning that I was prioritizing and completing the tasks that were the most important under a very, very high workload. I gave the best that I could under the circumstances - I needed to do what needed to be done for the good of the organization.

These were indeed the consequences of moving into a fast-paced business experiencing phenomenal growth but without the necessary resources to support this. This in itself seemed to be a major challenge for existing employees, let alone a new employee with high expectations from the organization. I made my immediate manager aware of this feeling of this issue. Having been in a similar situation of starting a new job/role before—I could safely say that this was different—although the people in the organization probably would've normally spent hours training and explaining, they were under tremendous pressure too—they had little/not enough time for me. Although I was quite verbal about my exhaustion and state of mind to my immediate boss and needed "time out" I wasn't allowed this - this correlated with key deliverables in the business calendar. For my own state of mind, I had to make the bold move of "reporting myself" to HR (as I put it then) and at some point, I reported my unfortunate circumstances to HR and to the head of the organization. This was a necessity. My ethos throughout my career has been and still is that I need to always ensure that I am in a state to give nothing less than my very, very best and exhausted and close to insanity was not it. I felt that I was contributing to the organization as I should; however, I wanted to be able to do even more.

I was relieved that finally I had sympathetic ears who seemed genuinely interested in listening and in exploring avenues to make my tenure at Terminus less painful. I was assured that the organization was aware of the serious issues within the total marketing team and were exploring means to ease the frustration and workload. My understanding was that the full Executive team was well aware of the circumstances and were exploring means of dealing with this. This was somewhat therapeutic.

In the meantime, the situation would stay the same until a viable solution was determined and implemented. The marketing team continued to operate in crisis. Apart from my situation, the brand team was experiencing serious challenges in terms of workload and with the leader, which they indicated they had reported at the forums that were presented. I had also reported my challenges with my immediate manager to HR and had tried to use what I had learnt in previous leadership courses and the Enneagram system to "manage upwards". I was taking responsibility for my part of the relationship and trying to make this work. I don't think that my intervention worked. One of the most disappointing incidences at Terminus was the treatment that I received from my immediate manager and the inferences made at some points that my behaviour would be and is determined by virtue of my race, in the negative sense, the ultimate insult for any person of colour. My discussions around my possible (or planned departure at that stage) were managed in the most surprising of ways, which ultimately resulted in the demand for my written resignation—a first for me.

Previous experience in the organizations at which I have been employed have been quite the contrary, especially since I have always tried to ensure that my departure from any organization is an amicable and "pleasant" one. The reasons given by both HR and my manager at the time was that I had verbally indicated an intent to leave the organization and was therefore bound by law to put this in writing and leave Terminus after the set 2 months' notice, which I subsequently confirmed is not true. I was informed that the date of my departure was in the hands of my immediate manager because I had uttered an intent of possibly leaving Terminus. This was not leaving me nor my family any room for retrospection at all which is a human trait.

The legal minds in my circles were in shock. Those who know me and have worked with me and understand my work ethic and value system were even more shocked! For someone who intended to have a long-standing relationship with the organization this needed to be dealt with professionally and truthfully. My manager's reasoning was that I needed to leave then because I wouldn't be committed and would not contribute as I should. The words uttered were: "Be honest with yourself...". This triggered and reminded me of an utterance made when one of the black ladies that have left marketing had resigned. Being honest with myself to me means being true to the track record that I have set in the many years that I have invested in my career. My track record in terms of exiting organizations speaks for itself. It is not in my nature to leave any organization without fulfilling my duties. This was an unfair statement. When I sat back and reflected on this incident it reminded me of what had happened a few months prior to a young black lady who had formally reported a similar scenario to me. She had complained of being forced to resign...I understand much more clearly now. Is this a trend?

To "add insult to injury" is the use of the word "STUPID" in reference to an individual or an idea that they have proposed – THE ULTIMATE. Sadly, this is the term allegedly used by my immediate manager to express her thoughts of one such idea from myself and one of my Black subordinates. Upon hearing this, I could not help but shake uncontrollably at the prospect of moving a few decades back. The oxford dictionary has a definition for this term; however, this is an insult in any one's book with an impact that is far reaching than the orator could possibly imagine. It is words such as these that are destructive and have a long-term impact on people's confidence. I am reminded of the stories that our grandparents told us as kids and continue to remind us of where they were addressed as "STUPID" and treated as "STUPID". Yes, we are black, but we are decent human beings trying to make a difference and do not deserve to be addressed or treated in that way. Our blood is red, we have veins and a heart, but most importantly, we have feelings, destructive words cut to the core of our being and hurt us deeply.

There are several examples that can be raised; however, what needs to be highlighted is my major concern, the negative trend in marketing of not retaining black talent. I strongly believe that not enough has been done to protect the interests of Black individuals within marketing at Terminus. This has been further amplified by the experiences of a brilliant young black lady who has joined the organization and who is experiencing the same issues as myself, despite doing all that is within my power to assist.

When she joined the organization, I was ecstatic as I believed that she represented the future of Terminus. Another amongst many that would follow in Terminus's quest to capture the hearts of SA and to entice Black talent in support of this. This concern was raised with the head of the organization. There seems to be something wrong with the equation, with the pattern. How does it happen that capable individuals with seemingly good track records, selected from amongst many, could be reduced to this?

The organization is on a quest to capture the hearts of Black South Africans through demonstrating and fostering the spirit of "Ubuntu", fostering care through Project Lerato. In my opinion, to implement this campaign whilst treating Black South Africans within the organization (in marketing) in the manner that they have been and are being treated would be an insult to Black South Africa. The fact that this would be driven by the marketing department makes it all the more concerning given the circumstances, previous and existing. The authenticity of the campaign in terms of the intent is already lost, a contradiction. "Ubuntu" may be a novelty, a concept that may receive worldwide acclaim in the Terminus world globally; however, to me and many others out there, this is what we as Black South Africans hold dear, what we have lived throughout our lives and continue to live as it evolves. To see it depicted in this fashion is painful...it feels more like a representation similar to costume jewelry, Shiny, Bright and "Real" on the surface and yet lacking depth and authenticity in the inside. How could this possibly be right? The treatment of people on the inside needs to reflect the Terminus values, particularly the CARE... that aptly reflects what "Ubuntu" is about.

And so, as I open the next chapter in my book, in my journey I can't help but wonder.... Who's Next?

I still believe that this is a great organization, I believe in the current leader (who has a heart and genuinely cares); however, I strongly believe that more could be done to protect and nurture the talent that is sourced. Not much can be done for me, my tenure at Terminus is almost over; however, I hope that this kind of story is never to be repeated...

Many thanks & My best regards,"

This is an example of a heartfelt letter that ignited a change in the trajectory of an organization, opening doors for existing employees and those who joined thereafter. One may argue that the option to speak out is one only followed through by the brave, given the offensive brutality that is expected when one speaks up against the Pitbulls of this world. How then do we collectively break the continuing reign of Pitbulls in corporate South Africa and the cycle of destruction on black families and communities?

My belief is that if we want to create a future where our children and future generations can thrive on the same playing fields as all other races, we have no other choice but to continue to deal with discrimination and bullying head on, just as our forefathers did for us.

ALUTA CONTINUA...

EPILOGUE

As an avid traveller I have observed how meticulous and involved the process of preparing, executing, and living through each and every trip that one takes across the globe from airport to airport. The preparations on the other end of the spectrum which include the pilot, groundsman, airport staff and many others is even more meticulous than that of the traveller and should leave very little room for error which is why the title: "Perfect Landing. Wrong Airport" should ring an alarm immediately. For the traveller all the flight travel processes are already so intimidating as you go from sourcing visas then from checkpoint to checkpoint until you successfully make it through into the intended destination. It is indeed the ultimate disappointment to arrive at the destination only to discover at some point that you've landed at the wrong airport.

This is where the analogy relates to my corporate journey, where I went through all the selection processes to assume certain key roles only to find that I was stepping into "land mine infested" terrain, in a hostile environment, a war zone that did not embrace diversity wholly and was not ready to embrace and protect black women of excellence.

This experience, "Perfect Landing. Wrong Airport" is not the experience of one woman; however, it is the story of many other black women in corporate who need to find their voices and to heal through sharing their stories, including the lessons learnt, with others. Racial discrimination still exists in corporate and needs to be dealt with, one bite at a time. "Perfect Landing, Wrong Airport" is meant to help in paving the way.

ABOUT THE AUTHOR

Born and raised in humble beginnings by Ruth Thozama and Frank Charles Ford, Dr Ella Ford Mthethwa is a proud product of Machibisa Township which forms part of Greater Edendale in Pietermaritzburg. She credits her solid grounding not only to her family but also from the lessons learnt through the hard-working women and men in the community who really epitomized the spirit of "Ubuntu". In a community that didn't have much, she fondly remembers how sharing and caring for each other as a collective was common. In her words: "The community safeguarded and protected each other to such an extent that even the local "tsotsi" (criminal) would send us on our way home immediately if he found us loitering outside after the streetlights came on." The spirit of oneness and humaneness experienced in her formative years is what she has lived and carried into her corporate life and

and has been a key driver in the extensive work that she has done as a Humanitarian.

Dr Ella Ford Mthethwa is the founder of Ellagence Wellness Boutique & Foundation (NPO), an organization on a mission to build healthy communities across South Africa and beyond, through holistic health and wellness initiatives, empowering families to work together to prevent lifestyle diseases in order to raise children who are healthy, well balanced and reach their full potential. Over the years her work has extended into corporate wellness where she has been involved in employee wellness programmes and has been active in driving the cause for attaining as well as maintaining the physiological well-being and psychological safety of employees in the workplace.

Apart from her vast experience in Corporate with responsibilities in Africa, USA and the Middle East, she is a Health Professional, an Entrepreneur, Healthy Lifestyle Coach, a Motivational Speaker, Multimedia Contributor, Freelance Writer, an Author and a South African Military Veteran who is often called upon to share her wisdom on various topics across local and global platforms.

She has been involved extensively through Ellagence in programmes for women, the youth and families which has led to collaboration with global organizations. She is a National Director for the International Youth Society SA and is the Chairperson for LOANI (Ladies of All Nations International) SA which has over 180 member countries. She is also a member of the World Public Health Nutrition Association and the Commonwealth Entrepreneurs Club.

In her journey she has been honoured with several corporate awards as well as those from globally acclaimed organizations. She was awarded Mrs Uniworld Business-woman of the Year, Mrs Intellect and Mrs Fitness in 2019 and has been celebrated as an Influential Woman of the

Year 2018 & 2020/2021 amongst various awards.

One of her highlights is that she has been honoured by The Nelson Mandela Foundation as part of their 2020 Women's Month celebration of women who are to be acknowledged whilst alive and are making a meaningful impact in society. She has also been bestowed with an Honorary Doctorate in Humanitarianism by the GIA Advocate University based in Berkeley Lake, Georgia - USA.

www.ingramcontent.com/pod-product-compliance
Lightning Source LLC
Chambersburg PA
CBHW050951050726
47592CB00007B/2522

9 780639 720418